MW01125020

HOW TO TALK TO ANYONE

Healthy Approach to Raise Confidence and Charisma, to Improve Communication and Social Skills, and to Master Small Talk

PAUL NEWCOMER

TABLE OF CONTENTS

INTRODUCTION

Some time back, my cousin Emma told me about the time she landed her first real job. She was fresh out of college and ready to tackle the challenges of the corporate world, armed with nothing more than a degree and a smile. That smile vanished quickly when Emma realized she was swimming far outside of her comfort zone.

As soon as the conversation strayed beyond the obligatory "How do you do?" Emma had no idea how to interact with unfamiliar people. Her mind would become a wasteland filled with anxiety. Her only thoughts were, *What do I say now?* Needless to say, Emma's work colleagues did not remember much of their conversations, especially after meetings or social functions. They'd usually describe the encounter with Emma as one that was filled with awkward silences, uncertain body language, and generic small talk.

"The supervisor even called me into his office to talk about my confidence. He's got it wrong though; my confidence is not the problem. I just don't know what to say to people or how to get them to listen to me," Emma would lament. I told her the same thing that I'll tell you now: "A touch of confidence is the magic ingredient that makes speakers so memorable."

Confident speakers can captivate an entire room of people simply by being themselves. Confidence is not some gift bestowed to us by the gods, unlike what most of us are led to believe. It is a skill. One that we can hone with patience and practice. I know this from experience because I was a lot like Emma.

Meeting new people was hard, so my dating life was a wasteland of missed opportunities. Speaking to new people was a tough, messy business, as I never could tell if people actually listened to what I had to say. Most of the time, talking to people would leave me feeling sweaty and on the verge of panicking, but eventually, I realized two things that would change the way I think about communication forever.

Since communication is a skill that we learn, the more we practice it, the better we'll get at it. This book will help guide you as you embark on your journey. First, we'll need to cultivate the right mindset so that we are in the right mental space to meet new people. After that, we'll tackle challenging topics such as starting a conversation in different contexts, becoming more charismatic and confident, and how to avoid certain social faux pas.

By fostering connections with those around us, we'll be able to uncover more opportunities to practice our communication skills. With enough practice and patience, these skills will become second nature.

Of course, when we are making a change in our lives, it is best to focus on our education and awareness in addition to practice. Education helps us make informed decisions. I'm not talking about the school brand of education, where we are told what to study. I'm talking about nurturing an awareness to apply what we learn and to learn from our mistakes. Through education, we can discover where our shortcomings lie and where we need to improve our speech to sound more convincing. This level of improvement takes some time and patience, but it can be achieved!

In every conversation, there seems to be a person that dominates. Perhaps you know a person who can speak about anything to anyone, confidently carrying the conversation in any situation. But these masterful communicators had years of trial and error etched into them. Years of making a social faux pas, awkward encounters, and practicing new delivery techniques. Each experience only added to the confidence and charm that they exuded now, but they would have had embarrassing conversations and awkward silences at some point in their lives. Nobody is born with perfect communication.

Having dedicated countless hours to understanding and refining communication skills, I've become well-versed in the intricacies of interpersonal interactions. I've witnessed firsthand the abundance of advice available on the internet. While some of these tips may seem helpful on the surface, many fail to foster healthy communication habits. Through trial and error, I discovered that several of these tips not only failed to improve communication but also, in many cases, caused more harm than good. This realization led me to understand the importance of empathy and a genuine connection with others as the foundation of effective communication.

During a particularly introspective period in my late 20s, I came to terms with the fact that my life was quite unfulfilling. Despite a successful career and an exciting urban lifestyle, I lacked meaningful friendships and connections. I realized that my inadequate communication skills were limiting my personal and professional growth, causing me to miss out on invaluable opportunities.

Determined to make a change, I committed to mastering the art of communication. I immersed myself in extensive research and applied the knowledge I gained to my own life. Though the journey wasn't always smooth, my setbacks served as invaluable learning experiences that shaped me into a person with a strong grasp of interpersonal communication.

Now, with a deep understanding of healthy communication practices and armed with my own experiences, I am prepared to help you acquire the essential skill of talking to anyone. The world is teeming with opportunities for engaging conversations, from casual exchanges at the bus stop to leading critical board meetings. The only remaining question is: Are you ready to embrace the transformative power of effective communication?

CHAPTER ONE:

WHY AND HOW TO START

---

*"Good communication is as stimulating as black coffee,
and just as hard to sleep after."*

— ANNE MORROW LINDBERGH —

We are communicating all the time, whether it is
texting a friend, writing an email, or trying to introduce
ourselves to someone new. Conversations used to be
stressful for me. I did not know where to start or how
to continue a conversation. That all changed when I
understood its importance. Communication is the
essence of life and, by extension, an expression of love.
I say this because the effects of poor communication
are easily seen in the elderly. They are often stressed,
anxious, and depressed as a result of the poor

communication that exists between themselves and their family (Ghazavi et al., 2016).

Just think about it for a moment. At their best, our interpersonal relationships can be wonderful sources of stress relief. Being able to talk to a friend or loved one about the things that bother us is cathartic (Scott, 2020). In return, our friends and loved ones turn into a source of support, helping to keep our mood bright and stress levels low. When we struggle to communicate or use a poor style of communication, stress can result. This type of stress is often a constant, low-grade type (Scott, 2020). Of course, a lack of self-esteem could hinder our ability to communicate; more on this in Chapter 2.

There are practical needs for communication, too. It is a basic need, especially when we look at communication through the lens of Maslow's hierarchy of needs. If you're not familiar with Maslow's hierarchy, here's a quick crash course. Maslow represents people's various needs in a hierarchical pyramid. At the bottom level of the pyramid, we find basic physiological needs such as food and sleep. These basic needs are essential for our physiological functioning, and when we've met them, we can address needs higher up in the pyramid. People communicate to satisfy their needs higher up on the pyramid, making it a basic need and an essential skill to develop (Wrench et al., 2020).

Components of Quality Communication

Did you know that there are four components that facilitate good communication? These components are confidence, genuine interest, the ability to read social cues, and the ability to adapt to your audience. Without these components working together in harmony, it can become tricky to share our ideas. So let's take a closer look at the pillars that support quality communication.

- CONFIDENCE: If someone is shy or socially anxious, or if a person is excessively self-aware or possesses negative, inflexible beliefs about themselves, it can make it challenging to practice communication skills, such as engaging in conversation with others. Therefore, if shyness and social anxiety are obstacles to communicating with others, it is advisable to address these issues first.

- GENUINE INTEREST: Actions speak louder than words. If we don't show others we are interested in the conversation and genuinely care about what they have to say, communication becomes difficult. When we are self-conscious or preoccupied with our thoughts, we rob ourselves of a potentially stimulating conversation. Active listening is crucial to having great conversations.

- READING SOCIAL CUES: Reading social cues allows you to understand how the other person is feeling and reacting to what you're saying. It helps you adjust your communication style to make the other person feel more comfortable and engaged in the conversation. Moreover, reading social cues helps us avoid uncomfortable situations, because we'll notice when someone wants to end the conversation or change the topic. Reading social cues shows that we are attentive and empathetic, which goes a long way to build rapport.

- ADAPTING TO YOUR AUDIENCE: Different people have different communication styles, values, beliefs, and cultural backgrounds. Failing to adapt to these differences can result in misunderstandings and even conflicts. Adapting to your audience involves tailoring your message, tone, language, and approach to best suit the needs and preferences of the person or group you are communicating with. For example, when explaining a complex idea it is best to avoid jargon and use simple language.

TIPS TO BEAT CONVERSATIONAL ANXIETY

Anxiety may stem from the worry of being judged, criticized, or embarrassed. On the flip side, being the center of attention can spark anxiety, as well. Just imagine how that will impact a person's performance at their workplace. After all, communication is an important skill. Well, it turns out that the impact can be significant. Studies have found that a lack of effective communication in the workplace can have an impact on mental health (SHIGEMI et al., 1997). Interestingly, effective communication is not only linked to creating an innovative work environment but is also correlated with work safety (Parker et al., 2001).

A study published in the *Journal of Occupational and Environmental Medicine* took the significance of quality communication in the workplace a step further by investigating the impact of communication skills training in the work environment. The participants, doctors, and nurses who worked in medical settings were given communication skills training based on the principles of cognitive behavioral therapy. The results were quite impressive, leading to improved relationships between healthcare providers and patients, which increased satisfaction levels for patients and their families (Sasaki et al., 2017).

Conversational anxiety can make it difficult to communicate. We might tell ourselves things like, "I'm no good at small talk," or "I'm socially awkward," but these unhelpful thoughts can be overcome with cognitive restructuring. This way of thinking helps us realign our thoughts to make them more helpful, self-compassionate, and realistic. The tips that follow will help you with some of these unhelpful behaviors.

UNHELPFUL BEHAVIOR: AVOIDANCE

This behavior can manifest in many ways, such as not attending activities, refusing to initiate conversations with people, not joining in on group conversations, or speaking little about yourself. I used to be hesitant to express my opinions or would often cut conversations short. These behaviors are designed to divert attention away from us and can be observed in our body language, such as avoiding eye contact. While we may feel better for a few moments as a result of doing these things, avoidance can contribute to our anxiety in social situations in the long run.

REMEDYING AVOIDANCE

I find that setting frequent, small goals to move beyond our comfort zone can be a useful force to help us participate in activities that we've been avoiding. The secret is to focus on the person, activity, or conversation we are involved in. But it does not end there. We need to repeat these goals until we've become comfortable with them. Over time, we can gradually make these goals more challenging.

Taking small, frequent steps forward helps us build self-confidence, and shows us that our unhelpful thoughts, such as "I'm no good at small talk," can change.

UNHELPFUL BEHAVIOR: SCRIPTING

Ever tried to figure out what you were going to say before you said it? That's called "scripting." On occasion, scripting can be useful; like when we need to explain our thoughts in detail. However, scripting also distracts us from listening actively to the conversation, disrupting its natural flow.

REMEDYING SCRIPTING

Rather than worrying about having a response ready, it is best to focus on what is said in the moment. Simply continue to pay attention to the speaker and be curious about the conversation; your brain will produce a response if you don't distract it with scripting. This is called "free association," and can make for wonderful, fulfilling conversations!

Social conversations naturally meander to different topics, so don't be afraid to change the topic if free association takes you there. Dropping the unhelpful behavior of scripting may feel scary at first, but trust in yourself. You have the ability to create wonderful conversations!

UNHELPFUL BEHAVIOR: GIVING BRIEF RESPONSES

Ever tried to have a conversation with someone but only received short answers in reply? It can be downright frustrating trying to have a conversation with someone who only gives short answers. This frustration is understandable, as it generally gives us nothing to work with when wanting to build the conversation. But there is a good reason why some people do this. The reason usually is to divert attention away from themselves, but it can give the impression that the person is taciturn.

REMEDYING BRIEF RESPONSES

If you're in the habit of giving short answers, try setting a goal to speak a few sentences at a time. Longer answers and telling stories are great ways to help make the conversation flow and build rapport (*Conversational Anxiety*, n.d.). When someone next asks, "How are you?" avoid saying the clichéd, "I'm fine, thanks." Try to elaborate. You could say something along the lines of: "I'm fine, but work has been hectic. So I'm really looking forward to the weekend. Maybe I'll sleep in or watch that new movie everyone's been raving about." A longer response gives the person you are talking to a lot more leeway to continue the conversation.

CHAPTER ONE KEY TAKEAWAYS

✓ Conversation is a fundamental human need. In fact, a lack of conversational skills can impact our mental health and contribute to workplace stress.

✓ Quality conversation rests on the pillars of confidence, genuine interest in what the other person is saying, adapting to your audience, and nurturing the ability to read social cues.

✓ Unhelpful behaviors such as giving short answers and scripting can make it challenging to connect with your peers. Focus on small, achievable goals to build self-esteem and improve communication skills.

CHAPTER TWO:

UNDERSTANDING YOURSELF

"When you are content to be simply yourself and don't compare or compete, everyone will respect you."

— LAO TZU —

What leads us to hide certain parts of ourselves? We all have reasons for doing what we do, and sometimes hiding parts of ourselves prevents us from being rejected in some way. After all, the need to belong is an important basic need according to Maslow's hierarchy of needs. So powerful is this need that research found that nearly half of the adults polled admitted to hiding their true selves from friends, family, and significant others (Brimble, 2021). That's some thought-provoking stuff. It's no secret that we all hide our true selves to some extent. The big question we need to ask ourselves is: Is wearing a mask helpful?

For years, researchers have tried to answer this question by focusing on what makes people likable. Is it body language (more on this in the next chapter), or something else? What they found was that being fake or ingenious does not help our likeability. That's because people are quite intuitive, and eventually, they'll catch on that we've been wearing a mask to fit in. When the people around us realize that we are hiding our true selves, they might lose respect for us since we do not have a secure sense of who we are (Mindnatic, 2022). So how can we develop a secure sense of self? We do this by understanding our perspectives and values.

THE INFLUENCE OF PERSPECTIVE

Our perspectives are formed from a lifetime of experiences, interactions, and education. Imagine a friend showing you a picture of a spider and asking you to adopt it through a heartwarming tale. How would you react? Chances are, if you are afraid of spiders, you won't even listen to the story your friend is telling!

Understanding our perspectives is the key to improving our communication skills. In addition to our perspectives, certain environmental and social factors can influence the way we communicate.

These factors include:

- ATTITUDES: This refers to a person's temperament and dictates how they would react to a topic, object, or idea. Attitudes tend to change often and easily (Gordon, 2022).

- BELIEFS: This refers to the way a person feels about something. Beliefs are usually based on past experiences and form the basis of how we interpret new ones. It should be noted that beliefs aren't always accurate and can be highly biased.

- VALUES: This refers to the significance we attribute to an object or idea. Values tend to influence our attitudes and beliefs and can be hard to change.

Our attitudes, beliefs, and values influence the way we see ourselves, but this can change over time.

EMBRACING YOUR AUTHENTIC SELF

To understand the influence that self-esteem may have on our work, relationships, schooling, and health outcomes, psychology professor Richard W. Robins and former postdoctoral scholar Ulrich Orth reviewed the findings of hundreds of long-term studies. Their findings revealed that people with high self-esteem perform better in school and at work, but that's not all the researchers noticed. They found that self-esteem is linked to better social relationships, improved physical and mental health, and less antisocial behavior (Orth & Robins, 2022). In the context of the study, "self-esteem" refers to self-acceptance and self-respect.

So how do the results of the study apply to us in real life? The majority of us worry too much about what other people think of us. As a result, we may hide or control aspects of our personality to make sure that people don't judge or react negatively to us. To gain acceptance, we might wear a mask, hiding our authentic selves. Being authentic requires us to be open and vulnerable.

Normally, our thoughts are a tangled mess of excuses as to why we can't do something. A lot of it has to do with self-esteem and the pursuit of "safe" communication. When we think to ourselves, "I can't say that," or "I don't want to step on any toes," or "Nobody cares how I feel," we might be doing more harm to ourselves than we realize. The minute we alter our thoughts and feelings to pursue a safer avenue of communication, we essentially limit our development (Schwartz, 2019). Remember, communication is key to fulfilling our needs and embracing our true selves, as we learned in the previous chapter. Suppressing our authenticity limits our ability to share our thoughts and experiences with the world. Low self-esteem is often a motivating factor for wearing a mask.

Seven Ways to Build Self-Esteem

Everyone goes through times when they find it hard to believe in themselves. When it becomes a long-term situation, it can lead us to experience low self-esteem. There are various causes of low self-esteem in people, not just the one I mentioned. Fortunately, there are ways we can improve our self-esteem and quiet that inner voice of discontent. Apply the following tips in your life and experience the difference it can make, not only to your self-esteem but also to your ability to express yourself confidently!

- Challenge your negative beliefs: We all have negative thoughts about ourselves from time to time. Your first big challenge is to identify and challenge the negative thoughts you hold about yourself. For example, if you find yourself thinking *I'm not a good speaker*, look for evidence in your life that contradicts that statement. You might find that you are an excellent speaker under certain circumstances, such as when giving a speech or when motivating a friend. Write down the negative statement about yourself and the evidence you found that contradicts it. Keep it as evidence and refer back to it to remind yourself that your negative beliefs are not true (*Improving Self-Esteem*, 2011).

- LOOK FOR THE POSITIVE: It is also recommended to write down positive attributes about yourself on that same page. Include the positive things people have said about you. When you feel the dark cloud of self-doubt casting its shadow over you, look at the positive things you wrote to remind yourself about the good that exists in you. This helps to create a positive inner dialogue, which is an essential aspect of building self-esteem. If you find yourself doubting yourself, or telling yourself that you are not "good enough," gently remind yourself that you are a worthwhile person. At first, you might find that you are slipping back into old habits, but with regular effort, you'll find yourself (and your inner dialogue) turning more positive.

- FOCUS ON BUILDING POSITIVE RELATIONSHIPS: Ever noticed how certain people or relationships make you feel better than others? That's probably because you've got a positive relationship with those people. Other people can make us feel bad about ourselves, or bring us down with a constant stream of negativity. It is best to avoid these individuals for the time being as you build your own self-esteem.

- BE KIND TO YOURSELF: You don't have to be perfect or feel good about yourself all the time. Self-esteem tends to vary in different situations and with different people, and that is absolutely fine. Learn to give yourself a break and embrace what you feel. We all have times when we find it harder to maintain a positive outlook on life. The key is not to be too critical of yourself. Try to avoid criticizing yourself to others as this can reinforce your negative views. Worse still, it can give others a negative (and most likely false) impression of you!

- LEARN TO SAY "NO:" When we have low self-esteem it can be hard to stand up for ourselves and say "no." This can lead to a domino effect of us becoming overburdened, more stressed, and having even lower self-esteem as a result. Developing our assertiveness is therefore a great way to improve self-esteem as it reduces the odds of us being overburdened and establishes clear boundaries.

- EMBRACE CHALLENGES: Taking on a challenge does not mean you have to do everything by yourself; by all means, ask for help when you need it, but you'll have to be open and willing to try something challenging. By succeeding you'll show yourself (and that negative inner voice) that you have it in you to face difficult situations. Pick something realistic, but achievable, formulate a plan for how you'll achieve this challenging goal, and set your sights on success! Remember that failure is part of the learning process, and that it does not define you.

Meaningful change takes time. The key is to keep your sights fixed on the future and focus on the big picture. When you feel good, celebrate it! If you find yourself slipping into negative thought patterns, gently challenge those negative thoughts and continue to build on your progress. Sooner rather than later, you'll find that your self-esteem has gotten a significant boost, and you may find yourself feeling a lot more confident in conversations.

CORNERSTONES OF A COMMUNICATION MINDSET

One technique I used to improve my communication was by looking at the observable skillsets of good communicators. How did these communicators tell stories to build rapport? How did they share their vision? I wanted to unravel the secret behind their effective communication when I noticed a common theme: These communicators had the right mindset. Without understanding and adopting the right mindset, we tend to fall short of becoming effective and authentic communicators (*The Mindsets of a Great Communicator*, 2021).

Mindset lays the foundation for the application of skill sets. This is where many books and courses on communication miss the bus, as they tend to jump straight into these skill sets. Keep in mind that we'll need to invest time and effort into nurturing the right mindset that will help us connect with others easier. The cornerstones below will help guide you on the right path.

- NURTURE HUMILITY: To foster this humbleness we need to respect the fact that we don't have all the answers. We need to learn to accept and recognize that other individuals have insights and perspectives that differ from our own. These perspectives and insights are valuable nonetheless! Nurturing humility allows us to be active listeners, to ask questions, and helps us adapt to our audience—all very important communication skill sets.

- DEVELOP CURIOSITY: When we display an interest in the conversation, the people we are speaking to become more engaged. When combined with humility, healthy curiosity communicates a sincere interest in the views and opinions of those around you. Next time you're in a conversation, try asking yourself *How does the speaker's background influence the way they feel about the topic of discussion?* or *What did the speaker mean when they said that?*

- PRACTICE EMPATHY: Empathy allows us to walk a mile in someone else's shoes. Asking yourself questions like, *How might this topic of discussion impact the other person?* will help you develop deeper empathy or understanding of the other person's feelings and experiences. It also encourages us to tailor our communication style to better connect with the people we are talking to.

- FOCUS OUTSIDE OF YOURSELF: Effective communicators are selfless and concentrate on the agenda of the other person, including what they're trying to accomplish, what they need right now, and how you might help them. Let's say we've met two people at a party. The first person talks endlessly about his own successes, goals, and hopes. The second person takes the time to ask about our preferences, worries, and objectives. Which person will encourage more engagement and connection? The second, no doubt. That's because exceptional communicators pay attention to what the other person wants. They realize the exchange is not about them, but that it is a mutual give-and-take.

- BE WILLING TO IMPROVE: It takes work to communicate well. We need to pay attention and expend effort to actively listen and to ask open-ended, awareness-raising questions. Without it, you'll likely adopt a self-centered style of communication, devoid of humility, curiosity, and empathy.

OVERCOMING THE FEAR OF TALKING TO OTHERS

In the previous chapter, we explored ways to overcome conversational anxiety and the unhelpful behaviors that contribute to it. In this section, we're going to expand on this foundation by exploring ways we can overcome excessive shyness. In addition to what we learned about avoidance, scripting, and giving short answers, we can apply the following tips to help keep shyness in check.

- ACCEPT YOUR SHYNESS AND BE HUMBLE ABOUT IT: Don't ignore shyness if it's having a negative impact on your life; embrace it and be honest about the need for change. Shyness is frequently uncomfortable and embarrassing, but cultivating the humility required to acknowledge a problem is the first step toward meaningful change (Bindamnan, 2023).

- NURTURE THE RIGHT MINDSET: To effect any desired change, you'll need to embrace the appropriate mindset. Instead of trying to absorb all the information out there about ways to beat shyness, realize that your time is precious and that you need to be deliberate and patient in your efforts to change your temperament.

- UNDERSTAND THAT CHANGE TAKES TIME: Personal transformation is not a linear process. Most of the time it is random and iterative. On one occasion, you might conquer your shyness, and on the next, you might fail to do so. This is normal and you should not be hard on yourself. Be patient and keep working on small gains.

The process of overcoming shyness starts with acceptance, followed by a willingness and commitment to change that aspect of yourself. In time, you'll discover that the shyness lessens and that it becomes easier to express yourself to other people.

Keep in mind that there are many different kinds of communicators. There is no one-size-fits-all solution when improving communication skills. Some skills and tricks will suit you, and some won't. The key is to be open and willing to experiment with different things and to build your self-esteem along the way.

CHAPTER TWO KEY TAKEAWAYS

✓ Our perspectives have a big impact on the way we view ourselves, and as a result, can impact our self-esteem.

✓ Embracing the communication mindset and gently challenging the negative beliefs we hold are effective steps we can take to improve our communication skills and combat excessive shyness.

✓ Understanding the cornerstones of a communication mindset can help us become better communicators as we build our self-esteem along the way.

CHAPTER THREE:

BODY LANGUAGE

"The most important thing in communication is hearing what isn't said."

— PETER DRUCKER —

Have you ever misinterpreted someone's text message? It's happened to me a few times. Perhaps you felt the message was critical of something you did when, in reality, the writer had no such intentions. There is more to communication than just the words we use. Our body language, facial expressions, and voice tonality all have a big impact on how people interpret what we say.

The relevance of verbal and nonverbal cues was a topic of interest for psychologist Albert Mehrabian. In his 1967 research, Mehrabian looked at different combinations of "positive," "neutral," and "negative" attitudes as demonstrated by voice inflection and facial expression. He would test people's ability to assess others' emotions. Participants were asked to assess the speaker's attitude solely based on the tone of voice. After conducting his research, Mehrabian came to the conclusion that tone of voice and facial expression were the most important factors in circumstances involving feelings and attitudes (Mehrabian and Ferris, 1967).

The importance of the words themselves in communicating was minimal, as most of the meaning was conveyed nonverbally (*Mehrabian's Communication Model*, n.d.). It should be noted that the study only dealt with communication situations involving feelings and attitudes, but the findings helped give rise to Mehrabian's communication model. His emphasis was on the significance of these nonverbal "clues" when they appeared to be in conflict with the spoken words and/or tone. Mehrabian developed the 7-38-55 rule based on the results of his studies. Essentially, the 7-38-55 rule implies that:

- 7% of face-to-face communication is done through spoken word.

- 38% of our communication relies on a nonverbal component such as the tone of voice used.

- 55% of communication rests on body language.

Interestingly, Mehrabian's findings had very practical applications in the field of negotiation research. Former FBI hostage negotiator Christopher Voss applied the body language expert's findings to the field and found it a valuable tool to prevent misunderstandings during formal negotiation situations (Voss, 2021). Of course, we could consider any communication situation as an opportunity for negotiation. It is a negotiation of ideas and perspectives, and for that negotiation to be successful, all parties involved will ideally benefit from the mutual gain.

Simply put, if you are only listening to spoken words during a conversation, you are missing most of the conversation! When we don't pay attention to body language, we'll misinterpret what the other person is saying and miss precious opportunities to de-escalate a heated debate.

The next logical question would then be, "How do you apply the 7-38-55 rule in a conversational context?" The pointers below will help you with that.

- WATCH HOW THE OTHER PERSON IS BEHAVING: The 7-38-55 rule notes that the majority of meaning is conveyed nonverbally. In other words, how you say something is far more significant than what you say. Part of successful communication is to look for opportunities to ease the tension when it arises. For example, if a person becomes visibly agitated and starts raising their voice during a discussion, resist the urge to raise your voice, as well. This will only trigger the person to become more agitated. By remaining calm and speaking in a calm tone of voice, you'll help defuse the situation and prevent a heated debate from turning into an ugly argument.

- PAY ATTENTION TO NONVERBAL CUES: Sometimes discrepancies arise between spoken language and nonverbal cues. For example, if a friend smiles and says "I'm feeling fine" in a deadpan voice and breaks eye contact, we normally see it as a clue that something is not quite right. The words that were spoken did not match their body language. It could be that the friend chose to wear a mask to deal with a difficult situation (like we discussed in the previous chapter), or it could be something else. Paying attention to nonverbal cues, therefore, gives us valuable clues to what people are feeling.

- LISTEN TO THE TONE OF VOICE: The 7-38-55 rule states that voice tone contributes 38% of the meaning in communication situations. This means that learning to control your tone of voice can make you a better communicator! Different tones of voice convey different messages to the listener. We must be able to adjust our tone of voice in order to be effective during conversations, conflict-resolution discussions, or problem-solving sessions. This is where active listening becomes crucial, as it allows us to adapt to the situation.

When we have a better understanding of nonverbal communication, our ability to successfully communicate improves. Using the 7-38-55 rule as discussed in the tips above can significantly increase your capacity to help you better understand the intentions and underlying emotions of the people you are speaking with.

BODY LANGUAGE MATTERS

Body language impacts the way people perceive you. Whether we are going on a first date or a job interview, how we come across can make all the difference in communication. For example, positive body language tells others that we are open to new perspectives and that we are approachable.

Body language is frequently used in an unconscious manner. It's likely that someone will come across as uninterested and stressed if they are yawning in the meeting or tapping their fingers on the desk if their supervisor discusses the monthly sales targets. This can be remedied by simply adopting a better posture. This will give the impression that the person is more engaged and concentrating on what is being said.

Try to be more mindful of your body language, but don't let it stress you too much. If you have a habit of touching your forehead or cracking your knuckles, being more mindful of these behaviors will help you overcome these unfavorable nonverbal expressions. Body language should correspond to what you say and feel. So you should find feelings you want to show others and then add body language as an expression of them. Congruence is key.

MASTERING NONVERBAL CUES FOR IMPROVED COMMUNICATION

How we listen, look, move, and respond to people during a conversation lets the other person know whether or not we care, are being truthful, and how attentively we are listening. When our nonverbal cues line up with what we are saying, trust, clarity, and rapport result (Segal et al., 2022). However, when our nonverbal cues do not match our spoken words, it can lead to conflict, mistrust, and uncertainty. Developing your awareness of your own body language and nonverbal indicators is essential if you wish to improve your communication skills. There are different ways we can communicate nonverbally, including:

- FACIAL EXPRESSIONS: The face is incredibly expressive and can silently reflect a wide range of emotions. Facial expressions are also ubiquitous. For example, happiness is universally represented by a smile.

- BODY POSITIONING: Think about how a person's posture, gait, or the tilt of their head can influence how you see them. For example, shoulder shrugs are often used to relay to the other person that we don't know something. We often see this behavior in children when they are asked a question, they don't know the answer to.

- GESTURES: Our daily lives involve using gestures in one way or another. When debating or speaking excitedly, we might wave, beckon, point, or use our hands to express ourselves. Italians are famous for using their hands to punctuate what they are saying. Unlike facial expressions, the meanings behind some common gestures are not universal. You're out of luck if you believe that keeping your hands in your pockets will prevent any potentially offensive gestures from slipping out; in many countries, it is considered disrespectful to have your hands in your pocket when talking to someone (Vallin, 2022). Gestures, therefore, need to be used carefully, otherwise, they can contribute to misunderstandings.

- EYE CONTACT: Eye contact is a particularly significant kind of nonverbal communication because it is the most common sensory preference for most people. Looking at someone can convey a variety of emotions, such as attention, affection, attraction, or irritation.

Maintaining a comfortable level of eye contact can help to keep the conversation going, and it gives us a good idea of how much attention the other person is paying. On the other hand, too much eye contact (staring) can trigger discomfort.

- TOUCH: Humans use touch to communicate in a lot of ways. Consider the extremely different messages conveyed by, for instance, a shaky handshake, or a pat on the head.

- SPACE: Have you ever experienced awkwardness during a conversation because the other person was encroaching on your personal space? Although our needs for physical space vary, they are still there. How close or how far a person positions themselves from you can convey a variety of emotions, including intimacy, affection, hostility, and dominance.

- VOICE: People listen to what you say while also "reading" your voice when you talk. Your speaking volume, tone, inflection, and sounds that indicate understanding, are all things kids pay attention to. Consider the ways in which your tone of voice might convey confidence, adoration, rage, or sarcasm. Our speech rate matters, too. Normally, fast speech and a high pitch in the voice are perceived as less attractive or attention-commanding. Try to slow down your rate of speech and take care to enunciate words properly to clearly convey your meaning.

The internet is filled with advice on the "right way" to use body language. These sources might advise us to sit a certain way to project confidence or to steeple our fingers in some way. The reality is that these methods are unlikely to succeed. That's because we are constantly sending messages about our true thoughts and feelings that we can't control. Also, the more effort we put into controlling our body language, the stranger our signals are going to come across.

This does not imply that we have no influence over our nonverbal cues, though. For instance, we might cross our arms, avoid eye contact, or tap our feet in response to someone's message if we don't like what they're saying or disagree with it. Although we may not agree with or even like what the other person is saying, we can take deliberate steps to avoid sending the wrong signals by keeping an open mind and making a sincere effort to comprehend what they are saying, and why. This will help to prevent putting the other person on the defensive and foster open communication.

TIPS TO IMPROVE NONVERBAL COMMUNICATION

Successful nonverbal communication necessitates our complete attention in the present moment. It's guaranteed that we'll miss important cues if we are busy scripting what we'll say, are distracted by our phone, or are thinking about other things while someone is having a conversation with us.

By managing stress and increasing our emotional awareness, we can enhance our nonverbal communication in addition to being fully present.

MANAGING STRESS IN THE MOMENT

It becomes easy to misinterpret other people and give off unclear or unwelcoming body language when we are stressed. Keep in mind that emotions have the potential to spread quickly. The best course of action is to take a break if we feel overly stressed. Before leaping back into the conversation, it is advisable to take a moment to compose ourselves. Doing so will enable us to handle the situation positively once we've regained emotional equilibrium. Focusing on your senses, making use of calming movements, or deep breathing is quick and effective ways to reduce stress at the moment.

INCREASING EMOTIONAL AWARENESS

For nonverbal cues to be successful, we need to be aware of our emotions and how they affect us. Emotional intelligence can help us read and understand other people's body language and the sentiments behind it. As a result of being instructed to attempt to suppress our emotions, many people today are emotionally disconnected, especially from powerful emotions like anger, grief, and fear.

In all honesty, you can suppress or reject your sentiments, but you can't get rid of them. They remain and will continue to have an impact on your actions.

But you'll have more control over your thoughts and actions if you learn to connect with your emotions (even the negative ones) and increase your emotional awareness when compared to pantomime.

Researchers concluded that the temporal-orbitofrontal regions play a role in decoding the meaning behind expressive movements (Tipper et al., 2015). This region of the brain also plays a part in our learning processes. This is good news for those of us struggling to read the body language of others, as findings suggest that reading the meaning behind expressive movements and body language is a skill we can acquire like any other!

The next logical question would then be, "What are the steps I can take to learn this skill?" Once you've learned how to manage stress in the moment and increase your emotional awareness, you'll naturally become better at reading the nonverbal cues of others. It is also important to pay attention to the following:

- EYE CONTACT: Is the person making too much or too little eye contact?

- FACIAL EXPRESSIONS: Is the person's face mask-like and unexpressive or is their face filled with interest?

- TONE OF VOICE: Is the tone of voice used warm, confident, and filled with interest, or does it come across as strained?

- POSTURE: Are the person's body and shoulders stiff or relaxed?

- TOUCH: Does the person use touch to communicate? If so, is it appropriate to the situation, or does it leave you feeling uncomfortable?

The more you practice reading body language, the better you'll get at it. It is much better to observe and emulate the body language of people that you like. Don't try to control your body language too much; use it when you feel it is needed. Remember to be authentic, as discussed in the previous chapter; otherwise, your body language may come off as unnatural or as a mask.

CHAPTER THREE KEY TAKEAWAYS

✓ Not all body language can be controlled, but through mindfulness, we can bring unhelpful fidgeting under control.

✓ Emotional awareness and managing our stress at the moment are vital to mastering body language.

✓ Nonverbal communication can go wrong sometimes, sending messages we don't intend to the people around us. When this happens, we need to examine our body language.

✓ There's a wide variety of nonverbal cues ranging from the tone of voice, space, facial expressions, body positioning, eye contact, and gestures.

✓ Body language and nonverbal cues should always be congruent with what the person is saying, otherwise the message can come across as being inauthentic.

CHAPTER FOUR:

APPROACHING PEOPLE AND MAKING NEW CONNECTIONS

"Starting a conversation is like starting a fire - you need to create the right conditions for it to catch."

— VANESSA VAN EDWARDS —

When we are young, making friends can be as easy as sharing candy or gifting a "friendship bracelet." I doubt those strategies will have positive results for most adults since our social interactions become more complex as we grow older. Meeting someone new can be tricky, especially if we haven't put ourselves out there in a while. We might feel rusty and uncertain of what to say to the person we'd like to interact with.

There might be a worry nagging at the back of our minds that we may come off as strange or desperate. Sometimes we misinterpret a person's body language and assume they are open for conversation when they are not. This is what happened to Joel.

Joel was casually walking down the aisles of his favorite supermarket when someone caught his eye. The lady had her back turned toward him and wore a bright pink headset with cat ears. Joel thought it was amusing how she kept glancing from her notepad to the store shelves. She never made eye contact with anyone around her. Ignoring her closed body language, Joel decided to approach her and casually tap her on the shoulder. Immediately, the lady removed the headset and glared at him warily. He tried to start a conversation. The lady angrily told him that he was in a supermarket, not a hookup lounge. Needless to say, Joel learned a lesson in humility he would not soon forget. If only Joel knew when to approach someone, this social faux pas could have been avoided!

How to Tell if Someone Is Open for Conversation

As we can see from Joel's encounter, not all people are open to conversation. No matter how friendly and approachable we are, there are times when people won't be friendly back. There are three indicators we should be looking out for to prevent embarrassing situations like the one Joel found himself in. These indicators are quite reliable and inform us if a person wants to be left alone or not. The indicators include setting, context, and body language. Let's take a closer look at these indicators.

SETTING

More often than not, the setting we find ourselves in will reveal the purpose of our visit to other people. We visit different places for different reasons. Think about a coffee shop for a moment. Some people love to visit a coffee shop on their way home for a quick pick-me-up. Others visit the same locale to meet with friends or work on their latest novel. We might visit our local watering hole to catch up with friends or meet single people, a completely different activity and intention than visiting coffee shops or supermarkets. The purpose of our visit ultimately dictates whether we'd be open for conversation or not. Generally, when people are engaged in a solitary activity (such as writing or shopping), their body language will give us telltale signs that they are not open for conversation. We'll delve into body language a bit more at a later point.

We can't forget professional settings, either, like conferences. What do you think a person's intentions are when attending a conference? As most conferences are set up as networking events, it is safe to assume that people attending will be more open to conversation. So we need to be mindful of the setting we find ourselves in, as it is a big giveaway whether we'd be open for conversation or not.

CONTEXT MATTERS

After we've taken the setting into consideration, we need to take note of the context to judge if someone should be approached. We'll need to "read the scene" to determine if approaching a certain person will be fine. Take note if the person is sitting alone or with someone. Does the person look preoccupied or distracted? Does the person look relaxed, or are they busy typing away on a laptop?

Let's apply this to the following scenario: Someone you'd like to talk to is working on their laptop at your favorite coffee shop. How do we go about reading the scene? First, we need to take into consideration the setting. Coffee shops are known to be social hubs, so talking to people in this setting won't come off as strange. Next, we need to read the scene. The person in question is using their laptop to create a barrier between them and other people. Additionally, the person is sitting away from other people and seems very preoccupied. In this case, the context tells us that this person most likely won't appreciate being approached.

PAY ATTENTION TO BODY LANGUAGE

The final clue that tells us if approaching someone is fine lies in body language. As we discovered in the previous chapter, most of our communication is nonverbal.

When you learn to read body language accurately and combine that knowledge with what you learn from the context and setting, you'll be able to tell which people are approachable and which aren't. Pay close attention to the following:

FACIAL EXPRESSIONS AND EYE CONTACT

Someone who is open for conversation will likely have a relaxed or expressionless look on their face. Perhaps the lips will be turned upward in a slight smile. Most likely, this person will be looking around, paying attention to what people around them are doing, and will not avoid making eye contact.

If the person is not open to conversation, their facial expression might convey frustration, anger, or upset. They might be frowning, and their lips may be turned down or kept in a thin, straight line. Most likely, this person will be intentionally avoiding eye contact, for example, by looking away if you make eye contact or by looking down at their phone.

There are exceptions to everything in life. Some people have a neutral expression that makes them look angry or unapproachable. These people don't sport angry or unapproachable looks on purpose; they simply have what popular media refers to as "a resting bitch face." While the term may be comical, it highlights the importance of paying attention to the setting, context, and nonverbal cues before deciding to approach someone.

POSTURE AND MOVEMENT

Take a closer look at the person's posture and how they move their body. Are they sitting with their shoulders open and their torso turned toward other people? If so, it is likely that the person is open to conversation. Also, take a look at their hands if they are visible. If the hands are open, it is a good indicator that the person will be receptive.

If the person is facing away from others and has "closed" body language (folded arms and legs or clasped hands), it is likely that the person does not want to be approached and may be hostile to advances.

Keep in mind that crossed arms and legs could also indicate that a person is getting cold. Other people may find it more comfortable to sit with their arms and legs crossed, so we need to read these signals while paying attention to the context and setting.

SPACE

When a person does not intentionally create space between themselves and others, for example, by sitting far away from other people, it is generally considered a sign that they are interested in conversation. Of course, this cue needs to be observed in the context of the situation. A person seated close to others who are busy working on their laptop may not take kindly to being disturbed.

APPROACHING PEOPLE

It is true that body language communicates a lot about us, but it is hardly a one-directional thing! We can use body language to improve our mood. All you need to do is think of a time when you felt your most confident and adopt the body position that accompanied that feeling.

If you feel unsure about meeting or approaching new people, taking command of your body language to give you a confidence boost can help. There's research to back this up, and Amy Cuddy's body language study has been the subject of hot debate for quite a while now. The study focuses on the effects of power posing and was published in the journal *Psychological Science* in 2010.

The study aimed to investigate whether brief nonverbal displays of high-power poses (e.g. standing with arms raised and feet apart) versus low-power poses (e.g. slouching with arms crossed) can affect people's feelings of power and their levels of testosterone and cortisol (hormones associated with dominance and stress, respectively). Participants were assigned a high- or low-power posing condition for two minutes. Before and after the posing period, the researchers collected saliva samples to measure participants' hormone levels and asked them to rate their feelings of power and risk tolerance. The findings turned out to be quite fascinating.

Participants who had adopted high-power poses showed an increase in testosterone levels and a decrease in cortisol levels and reported feeling more powerful and willing to take risks than those who had adopted low-power poses (Carney et al., 2010). The effects of power posing were stronger among participants who were predisposed to feel powerless (i.e., those with low baseline testosterone levels).

The study suggests that adopting high-power poses for just two minutes can change people's hormonal levels and psychological states, potentially influencing their behavior in subsequent tasks. Simply put, body language has the potential to dictate how we feel. So, if we take the time to adopt a power pose for a few minutes, we may feel more confident! With our confidence boosted, it's time to work on how to approach people.

RESPECT THEIR PERSONAL SPACE

Personal space is basically the comfortable distance between you and another person when you talk or stand close to each other. Think of it as a personal bubble that protects you. If someone gets too close to you and invades your personal space, you might feel uncomfortable. For instance, when you're lining up at the store and someone stands really close behind you, nearly touching you, it feels downright uncomfortable.

People usually measure their personal space by the lengths of their arms. In gym class, you might have done this exercise where you stretch out your arms and move them around to make sure you're not standing too close to anyone. You have the choice to let someone into your personal space if you're comfortable with it, like when you want a hug from someone you know and trust, not a stranger. Personal space is important because it helps people feel at ease. The amount of personal space a person requires or desires varies depending on the situation, so we must keep this in mind.

When we approach someone and do not respect their personal space, we may come across as being combative. This is especially true when we approach people head-on rather than from the side or at an angle. We want the people we approach to feel comfortable in our presence, but a head-on approach may leave us looking combative.

EYES UP HERE

Having a meaningful conversation with someone requires establishing a connection by seeing "eye to eye." However, some people can make us feel uneasy due to the way they look at us or hold our gaze. Research suggests that when a person's gaze meets ours for more than two-thirds of the time, it can indicate that they find us interesting or appealing, with dilated pupils, or hostile and issuing a non-verbal challenge, with constricted pupils (*The Language of Eye Movements Part Two*, 2011).

Keep in mind that the length of time someone gazes at another person is determined by their culture. For example, Southern Europeans have a high frequency of gaze that might be considered offensive to others, and the Japanese tend to look at the neck instead of the face during conversations. It's important to consider cultural differences before making assumptions. Also, where you direct your gaze on a person's body and face can affect the outcome of a conversation. There are different types of gazes, which we'll briefly describe.

- BUSINESS GAZE: This gaze is usually used in serious discussions and our eyes are generally fixed on the person's forehead. Keeping our gaze directed at the forehead area creates a serious atmosphere. The business gaze usually does not dip below the other person's eye level.

- SOCIAL GAZE: Here, our gaze drops below the other person's eye level, creating a more relaxed and social atmosphere. This gaze tends to remain in a triangular area between the person's eyes and mouth.

- INTIMATE GAZE: This gaze is focussed across the other person's eyes and can dip below the chin to involve parts of the person's body. People use this gaze to signal their interest, and if the person is interested in return, they generally will return the gaze.

Using the appropriate gaze is important in different situations. For example, if a manager needs to reprimand an employee, using the social gaze might not be effective, while the business gaze can convey seriousness. So, understanding these different gazes can help improve communication skills in different situations.

USE THE POWER OF SMILE

Smiling is such a powerful gesture, but not all smiles are real. Many people use a fake smile to mask what they are feeling. But how can we tell the difference between the real deal and a fake smile?

The Duchenne smile (or real smile) is a result of two muscles working together. These muscles draw the corners of the mouth up and crinkle the outer edges of our eyes. A person who is wearing a fake smile typically won't have the crows' feet, but that is not the only way to tell if a smile is fake. Sometimes people try much too hard when forcing a smile, and in doing so, expose their bottom teeth in a big cartoony grin. Another way we can tell if a smile is fake is by taking the person's body language into account. Usually, people wear a fake smile when they feel uncomfortable in a situation but don't want others to know. Genuine smiles arise when a person is happy, relaxed, and having fun. However, if the person has tense body language while wearing a smile, this could be an indicator that they are trying to hide their discomfort with a fake smile.

MAKING YOUR APPROACH

We place so much pressure on ourselves when approaching someone, especially in the dating scene. I'm here to tell you that most of the time, that pressure is unnecessary. You don't need to be "slick," have "game," or employ tactics to approach someone. You just need to be your authentic self!

Still, this does not help us make the first move. We may feel like we are inconveniencing someone, holding them up, or interrupting them. We might feel hesitant to speak to strangers simply because we fear they might find us annoying. That's social anxiety rearing its ugly little head, but there is an actionable step we can take that may help in these situations.

We could indirectly approach someone for something, but we need to have this reason clear in our minds at all times. It shouldn't be a long-term reason either! If you find yourself thinking, *I want to talk to that person because I want to marry them*, know that you are putting way too much pressure on yourself. When we think like that, the chances of rejection hurting us increase, and we tend to focus too much on the outcome of the conversation. This can make us buckle under pressure when conversations become too much.

As with all things in life, it is the little things that count. When approaching someone, think along the lines of, *This person seems nice; I'll ask if they want to go for coffee later.* Asking someone to go for a coffee is a much smaller commitment, and will generate a lot less pressure.

The important thing to remember when approaching someone is to have a reason, even if we have to invent one. Inventing reasons to approach people is a fantastic way to exercise our social muscles, as it helps to unlock more possibilities to meet people. Some of the reasons we can invent to approach people to include asking them for the time, directions, or their opinion on something. Sometimes a simple, "Do you know anyone here?" is all that it takes to spark a conversation.

STARTING CONVERSATIONS IN DIFFERENT CONTEXTS

Starting a conversation can be a daunting task. What do you say to a person that you've just met or don't know well? It's a predicament I've found myself in quite a number of times. But with the right approach, starting a conversation can be a breeze. Let's explore some tips and tricks to help you start a conversation in different contexts.

PIVOT

One way to start a conversation is by pivoting. Pivoting is a technique that involves shifting your focus from one topic to another. If you are at a party and someone is talking about the weather, you could pivot the conversation by asking them about their favorite outdoor activity. This technique helps you move the conversation to a topic that you feel more comfortable talking about.

SIT IN A PLACE WHERE PEOPLE ARE LOOKING FOR CONVERSATION

You won't meet someone if you stay in your house the whole day, that much is true. The next time you head out, try to spend time in places that encourage conversation. This could be a spot at a coffee shop, a conference, or a party where people tend to gather. By sitting in a place where people are looking for someone to talk to, you increase your chances of starting a conversation.

In addition to these techniques, it's important to be genuine and authentic when starting a conversation. Try to be interested in the other person and ask open-ended questions to keep the conversation flowing. Starting a conversation can be challenging, but with the right approach, it can become a fun and easy task.

BODY LANGUAGE AND MICRO-EXPRESSIONS

Have you heard about micro-expressions? These occur when two or more people communicate; their body language can convey a message even before they say a word. According to body language expert Joe Navarro, nonverbal cues such as body orientation, posture, and facial expressions can indicate whether people are open or closed to others.

For example, if two people are standing face to face, but their shoulders are turned away from each other, it can indicate that they are not interested in interacting with others. Similarly, if two people are standing close together, but their feet are pointed away from each other, it can indicate a lack of interest or even hostility (Navarro and Karlins, 2015).

Moreover, body language can also reveal micro-expressions, which are brief facial expressions. These micro-expressions can reveal a person's true emotions, even when we are trying to hide them. I'll explain. Let's say someone is pretending to be happy but is actually feeling anxious or stressed. A micro-expression of fear or worry may briefly flash across their face (Matsumoto and Hwang, 2017). Similarly, if someone is trying to hide their anger or frustration, a micro-expression of disgust or contempt may briefly appear.

Understanding micro-expressions can be especially important in situations where there is a potential for conflict or misunderstanding. By being aware of these subtle cues, we can better understand others' emotions and intentions and adjust our own behavior accordingly. This makes body language a crucial aspect of communication, and it can reveal a lot about our intentions and emotions.

Using a Mentalist Trick to Start Conversations

Mentalists have always fascinated me, and I noticed that the very best of them had one thing in common: They've mastered the art of cold reading. Cold reading is a technique used by mentalists, psychics, and other performers to create the impression that they possess special abilities to read people's minds or predict their future. However, it can also be used in everyday situations as a way to start a conversation with strangers. Here are some tips on how to use cold reading to initiate a conversation.

Observe the Person
Before you approach someone, take a moment to observe them from a distance. Look at their clothing, accessories, body language, and facial expressions (Burger and Neale, 2018). These cues can give you clues about their personality, interests, and mood.

Start With a General Statement
Begin the conversation with a general statement that could apply to anyone. For example, "I get the sense that you're someone who enjoys trying new things," or "You strike me as someone who values independence."

Be Vague
When making statements, use vague language that can be interpreted in different ways. This creates the impression that you're saying something specific

about the person, when in fact, you're not. For example, "I sense that you have a creative side," or "You seem like someone who values deep connections with others."

PAY ATTENTION TO THEIR REACTIONS
As you make your statements, pay attention to the person's reactions. Are they nodding in agreement, or are they looking confused or skeptical? Use their reactions to guide the conversation and adjust your statements accordingly.

ASK OPEN-ENDED QUESTIONS
Once you've made a few statements, ask open-ended questions that encourage the person to share more about themselves. For example, "What kind of new things have you tried lately?" or "What does independence mean to you?"

DON'T OVERDO IT
Remember that cold reading is a tool for starting a conversation, not a way to manipulate or deceive people. Use it sparingly and respectfully, and be willing to switch to other conversation topics if the person seems uncomfortable.

Cold reading can be a useful technique for starting conversations with strangers. By observing their cues, making general statements, and asking open-ended questions, you can create a connection and learn more about the person. Keep in mind that cold reading will take some practice to perfect; misreads can happen, and remember to use this technique ethically and respectfully.

PROSOCIAL BEHAVIOR TO START CONVERSATIONS

Have you noticed that some people are simply easier to talk to? It could be that these individuals exhibit prosocial behavior. I'll explain. Prosocial behaviors are actions that benefit others in some way or are performed for the greater good. Some examples of prosocial behaviors include:

- Helping someone carry their heavy luggage.

- Holding the door open for others.

- Offering to help someone short on money at a vending machine.

- Giving up your seat on public transport.

- Letting someone with only a few items go ahead of you in a checkout line.

- Picking up something that someone has dropped and returning it to them.

These behaviors create opportunities to strike up a conversation with others. However, it's important not to overdo it or become manipulative by trying to create opportunities where they don't exist. Before approaching a group of people, it's important to first assess the situation and get a feel for how people are interacting with each other. By doing so, you can ensure that you communicate effectively and avoid any potential conflicts or misunderstandings. One way to improve your communication skills is to participate in various social activities, trying out different approaches and gradually building your confidence while reducing social anxiety.

There are many options for practicing, including activities such as games, restaurants, clubs, bars, courses, and even just going out on the street. It's important to try new things, step out of your comfort zone, and practice going alone instead of relying on a group. Additionally, social media and dating apps can provide opportunities to engage with others and explore different themes and topics.

CHAPTER FOUR KEY TAKEAWAYS

✓ It is possible to start a conversation in different contexts, whether you want to talk to someone who is part of a group or sitting on their own! Just be mindful of their body language and micro-expressions.

✓ Cold reading is a handy skill to learn and can help you connect with people more easily, but it should only be used with sincere intentions.

✓ Prosocial behavior (such as holding the door open or giving up your seat) is a great way to leave favorable impressions on the people around us, and it gives us opportunities to connect with others.

CHAPTER FIVE:

SMALL TALK

"Small talk is not small because it is unimportant. It is small because it is an entry point into a deeper conversation."

— JONATHAN FIELDS —

Did you know that almost every relationship we develop in our life starts with small talk? This easygoing and casual exchange typically takes place between friends, colleagues, and new acquaintances, and often involves discussions about unimportant or trivial matters. Although small talk may seem like a waste of time, it actually plays a significant role in establishing social connections and building relationships.

In fact, small talk is often used as a means of initiating more meaningful conversations and getting to know others on a deeper level. Research conducted by Patrick Downes, an assistant professor of management at the University of Kansas School of Business, shows that small talk can create a sense of connection and positive social emotions for individuals, making them feel like they belong (Methot et al., 2020).

Small talk is an essential part of our social interactions, especially when meeting new people (like we discussed in the previous chapter), plus they give us insight into the character of the speaker (Carnegie, 1936/2018). I could talk about my family, and this would give you a glimpse into my values and priorities. Similarly, if I discussed my work with you, you'd get a glimpse into what my skills and interests are.

Small talk is particularly important for people who are meeting for the first time, as it provides an opportunity to make a good impression and establish trust and respect. By engaging in polite and respectful conversation, individuals can lay the foundation for more authentic and meaningful interactions in the future. So, mastering the art of small talk is an important step in sharpening our communication skills.

MASTERING THE ART OF SMALL TALK

Small talk, just like any other skill, can be mastered with practice and patience. I've got good news for you, though: 99% of the battle is already won! You're already familiar with asking questions to keep a conversation going and observing a person to determine if you can approach them or not. That's the hardest part done. Now, you'll only need to work on your active listening skills (which we'll discuss in Chapter 6) and enthusiasm.

Researchers knew early on that enthusiasm was a powerful emotion and wanted to investigate its impact on social interactions. In 1957, a study examined the effects of enthusiastic behavior on social judgment, likability, and persuasiveness. The study concluded that enthusiastic behavior has a positive impact on social interaction and can make people more likable, interesting, and persuasive (Hinkle and Wolff, 1957).

How do the results of this study apply to us? By showing enthusiasm and energy during the conversation, we can help the other person open up, and in doing so, we are helping to create a deeper connection. Enthusiasm can make a difference in the most mundane of conversations. Try to recall a standard conversation you've had recently and imagine how this conversation could have been different if you showed three times the enthusiasm. How would that person react? Chances are, they'd return your energy with similar vigor, which can make for a stimulating conversation. Of course, you don't have to be enthusiastic all the time, but pick the time and place to add a little extra pep to your conversations.

INJECTING ENTHUSIASM INTO CONVERSATIONS

So, the million-dollar question now is: How do we go about it? Emulating enthusiasm can be hard, especially if you are not an energetic person. Showing excessive energy and enthusiasm beyond our normal limits may make us feel inauthentic. So how do we solve the problem of displaying more enthusiasm without coming off as fake? Fortunately, there are several ways we can go about this.

USE YOUR VOICE

The human voice is a wonderfully diverse thing. By using our voices to adjust tiny details in the way we speak, we can inject a considerable amount of energy into our conversations. We could speak a little louder, change our tone of voice, emphasize certain words, and adjust our inflection to make what we say fun to listen to. Take these two utterances as an example, and note that the emphasis falls on the capitalized words.

- "Horses are majestic. I rode one last weekend. It was amazing."

- "Horses ARE majestic! I rode one last weekend. It was AMAZING."

Notice how different the second utterance sounds from the first? By making tiny adjustments to the way we say something, we can inject a lot of emotion, energy, and power into our words. Of course, we can also use body language to amplify what we are saying and make the conversation more animated.

Don't Deny Your Feelings

In a conversation, there will be topics and ideas that resonate with us and some that we don't agree with. The great thing is that we don't need to agree with everything we hear to be likable. Whether you agree or disagree with a topic or statement, it is best to highlight how you feel. This helps us with two very important things: injecting energy into the conversation and being our authentic selves. So how do we highlight our feelings without coming across as pushy or offensive? The answer is an energy statement. Take a look at the following energy statements:

- "So, you are interested in that, too?"

- "I understand what you are getting at, but I don't quite agree. I prefer ABC."

See how much difference an energy statement can make? It allows us to express our feelings openly and honestly while being validating toward the other person. Energy statements can turn a placid and passive conversation into a direct and assertive one.

Mingle With the Right People

It is a fact that we won't be around positive, bubbly people every hour of every day. Nor does this prospect sound like a healthy thing. However, we need to mingle with people who have stable, positive attributes regularly if we want to adopt these personality traits ourselves (Williams, 2021).

Keep in mind that negativity is a very draining state of mind. It is incredibly hard to feel energetic when we are down in the dumps, so it is important to seek out and spend time with people who radiate uplifting energy and don't bring toxicity into our lives.

Exploring Small Talk Topics

Now that we know how to inject a bit of natural vitality into our conversations, we can take the next step and level up our conversation skills with small talk topics. The topics we can have a conversation about are as diverse as the human race, and while someone may care a lot about a given topic, another person might find it offensive. It is a tricky gray area that can leave us stuck with no way to move the conversation beyond the first, slightly awkward greeting. Fortunately, there are safe conversation topics hidden in our daily lives that we can discuss without upsetting anyone.

- Our immediate environment or the location we are in.

- Topics related to food, such as cooking, restaurants, or your favorite episode of *Hell's Kitchen.*

- Topics related to travel, holidays, and dream destinations.

- Sports, hobbies, art, and favorite local places are all great small-talk topics.

Sometimes, despite our best efforts, a conversation can become one-sided. There are many reasons for this. Researchers examined the relationship between social media use and perceived social isolation among young adults in the United States. The study found that higher social media use was associated with higher levels of perceived social isolation among young adults. Additionally, young adults who used social media for more than two hours per day were more likely to report feeling socially isolated than those who used social media for less than half an hour per day (Primack et al., 2017).

Social media prioritizes instant connections over building meaningful relationships. However, meaningful relationships don't just materialize in the real world like they do in young adult novels. You'll need to be patient and nurture the connection, but it will be worth the effort! If you find yourself at a loss over what to talk about, it's always a good idea to keep the following topics in your back pocket.

WEATHER

The weather is an easy and neutral topic to talk about, and makes for a great starting point, especially when you're just starting to master the art of small talk. Instead of asking the tired "How's the weather?" question, consider injecting a bit of energy and personality into the topic. We could say something like:

- "What beautiful weather. I wonder who ordered it?"

- "This fog is so eerie. It's like being in a fantasy novel. I love it!"

ENTERTAINMENT

Another staple of small talk is to talk about the things people enjoy doing in their free time. Whether it be the latest TV series, game, book, or that awesome fishing spot you know about, any form of leisure activity is a good discussion topic. Simply jump in and find out what people like. We could say something like:

- "Have you played Stray? What were your impressions of the game?"

- "Do you like sushi? There's a great sushi bar that opened recently. I've been dying to try their maki rolls."

PERSONAL LIFE

We should be careful about oversharing details about our personal lives with people we just met. This can come off as intrusive and forward. However, a few personal questions can help us get to know a person better. Examples of acceptable personal questions we can ask include:

- "Where did you go to school?"

- "Do you have siblings?"

- "Do you have pets?"

When asking personal questions, be sure to keep them non-invasive and respect the other person's boundaries. If you are still at a loss over what to talk about, you can talk about your career, hometown, or even pivot the conversation to celebrity gossip. The sky's the limit! Let the conversation evolve naturally and you'll do great.

TABOO TOPICS

Small talk topics can be considered taboo for a variety of reasons, including cultural, social, and personal factors. Some topics may be considered inappropriate or impolite to discuss in certain contexts, while others may be considered too personal or sensitive. Ultimately, what is considered taboo in small talk can vary widely depending on the situation and the individuals involved. Generally speaking, the topics that follow are reserved for conversations with people that we trust.

FINANCES

It is natural to be unwilling to answer if someone asks you how much you earn. It is an invasive question, and the contents of our answers are usually used to form a judgment on us as individuals. Judging and being judged are not healthy conversation starters and can leave a bad impression on the people we interact with. This topic should always be avoided.

RELIGION AND POLITICS

These topics will always ruffle a few feathers. It is best to save these until you know the person really well and a mutual level of respect and understanding exists. That way, both parties can freely share their ideas and feelings on the topics.

DEATH AND SEX

The topic of death can be very upsetting, making it incredibly hard to have a positive and uplifting conversation with someone. On the other hand, sex is a very personal thing. While there may be a time and place for a cheeky innuendo, in general, talking openly about sex with people we've just met can leave them with a bad taste in their mouths. If you want your initial meetings to leave a good impression, it is best to avoid talking about death and sex.

HEALTH ADVICE

Unsolicited health advice can be so annoying! Perhaps you can relate to this scenario: You're in a conversation and casually mention that you're feeling under the weather. All of a sudden, the other person jumps in and shares what herbal remedies you can use to feel better. I'm assuming this advice is given out of the goodness of their hearts, but in all honesty, this person is usually not a trained healthcare professional. It usually does not leave a favorable impression on people when health advice is foisted upon them, so do yourself a favor and don't be that person.

GOSSIP

Sharing a juicy tidbit about a celebrity is fine because these people choose to live their lives in the spotlight. Sharing gossip about your neighbor, coworker, or other people from your personal life is not fine. While gossip gets tongues wagging and fixes people's attention on you, it has the opposite effect of what we want. It makes people consciously avoid us just in case we end up gossiping about them.

OFFENSIVE JOKES AND APPEARANCE

While we can crack our most offensive jokes around the people we love, it is not advised to share offensive jokes with people you don't know. Doing so can land you in a world of trouble and alienate you from others. Just like we shouldn't make offensive jokes around strangers; it is best that we do not comment about physical appearance, either. That's because we don't know how sensitive a person may be about their own appearance. In either case, offensive jokes and commentary on physical appearance are in bad taste, and can quickly leave us alienated from the people we want to connect with.

DEAD RELATIONSHIPS

It is common knowledge not to talk about your ex when you are on a first date. That's because talking about these dead relationships will most likely turn the conversation into something negative. This negative connotation is not something we want to be associated with us when we are trying to form new bonds with people, so it is best to avoid talking about dead relationships. This includes dead friendships.

LIMITED TOPICS

Years ago, I encountered a gentleman with very limited conversational skills. He was a pleasant person, but he didn't have very many friends. The thing is, I don't think he was aware of how limited his conversations were. He'd speak passionately about how he spent his youth in England and about sports, even when other people had lost interest in the topic. Incessantly speaking about a topic other people aren't interested in is only a recipe to drive them away from you.

Moving Beyond Small Talk

Now that we've covered our bases with small talk, it's time to take the conversation to the next level. The goal is to shift the conversation to the other person so that you can learn more about them. As the conversation flows, we need to pay attention to changes in body language and show genuine interest (Borthwick, 2022). In this section, we'll take a look at the typical questions and topics that may arise when a conversation deepens and how we can approach them.

What Do You Do?

Repeat after me: Your job title does not define who you are. This is a mistake that many people make. Let's say you're a writer and someone asks you this question. You might reply with the standard "I'm a writer." But this answer does not really tell the other person what you do. There are many forms of writing, including copywriting, poetry, songwriting, and more. Simply stating "I'm a writer" does not give the other person anything to work with, because the answer is too vague.

How do we remedy this? By saying something along the lines of, "I write horror novels set in dystopian worlds. My current work in progress is about three kids trapped in an alternate dimension." This is a much more informative and interesting answer, and we created an opportunity for the other person to ask questions about our horror novel.

HOW ARE YOU?

Whenever this question arises, keep in mind that it is not our cue to start complaining or boasting. Everyone has their burdens, and we need to be mindful of that. In the same vein, if things are going very well for us, it is advisable to admit to some small challenges before delivering your good news. That's because we don't want other people to feel envious of our successes as that can push people away.

This example should make it a bit clearer: "I had a tough time starting my business. The clients didn't like the pastries I baked, but after changing the recipe, things are starting to turn around." A response like this gives a more balanced approach. We're not complaining, but we're not boasting, either.

ENOUGH ABOUT ME

When we realize that we've been speaking for too long, we can shift the conversation gracefully to the other person. Saying something as simple as "...but enough about me, I'd like to know more about..." gently shifts the conversation to the other person and gives them the opportunity to speak.

WHAT DO THE HEADLINES SAY?

It's always a good idea to stay abreast of what's happening in the world around us by staying updated on the news. It's worth looking into several news sources so that we can get different perspectives. Keeping up with the news may sound dated, but it can dent your credibility if a major event happens and you are unaware of it.

RESEARCHING AND ACKNOWLEDGEMENT

When meeting people who have specific interests or who work in a specific industry, it may be worth your while to refresh your industry knowledge a bit. There may be a current hot topic affecting that person's industry, and mentioning it will help to establish rapport.

On the other hand, if you know you are meeting a specific person, it will be a good idea to check out their social media accounts, blog, or website. The intention behind this is simply to find the information you can refer to in your conversation. For example, if you are meeting with your favorite author, you could mention which book, scene, or character you liked and the effect that their writing has had on you. This will help to build rapport and create a favorable impression of you.

"NICE" IS A LAZY WORD

If you want to build rapport with someone and pay a sincere compliment, avoid the word "nice" at all costs. It is a generic, unimaginative word that most people hear too many times in a day. Let's say the person we're talking to has vibrant red hair, and we want to compliment it. If we say, "Oh, your hair color is nice," it will give the impression that it's a generic response and that we've given no thought to what we're saying. Instead of using that naughty little "nice" word, we could say something more imaginative, like, "Your hair color reminds me of the sunset. It's gorgeous." See the difference it makes when we ban the "nice" word from our vocabulary?

Understanding Silence

Ever been in a conversation where the silence felt awkward? Silence is an intriguing aspect of human communication. It can be a source of discomfort, but it can also be a sign of respect or deep thought. A 2011 study dove deeper into the significance of silence by exploring the impact thereof on our social needs, perceived consensus, emotions, and rejection. The authors hypothesized that silences disrupt the flow of conversations, which can lead to negative emotions and feelings of rejection (Koudenburg et al., 2011).

Two experiments were conducted to test the hypothesis. The results suggest that conversational flow induces a sense of belonging and positive self-esteem. So how should one deal with that awkward silence in social situations? The tips that follow may be of use.

Accept That Silence Is Normal

Silence is a natural part of human communication. In fact, studies have shown that silence accounts for up to 30% of the time spent in conversations (Mehl et al., 2007). There are plenty of reasons why people remain quiet during a conversation, including the need to process information, shyness, or respect for the other person's thoughts and opinions. Silence can also be a way of communicating nonverbally, conveying emotions, or signaling agreement or disagreement (Okuhira and Yoshimura, 2016).

AWKWARD SILENCE AND NEW FACES

Meeting new people can be exciting, but it can also be nerve-wracking. One common challenge is dealing with awkward silences, which can arise when two people are unfamiliar with each other or have run out of things to say. I know I've felt a bit of discomfort and tension in those situations! One effective strategy for managing awkward silence is to ask open-ended questions. Open-ended questions are those that require more than a simple "yes" or "no" answer and encourage the other person to share more details. For example, instead of asking "Do you like your job?" you could ask "What's the best part about your work?" or "What inspired you to choose that career?"

LEADING TO WIDE ANSWERS

Another way to manage awkward silences is to lead the conversation to broad answers. This involves asking follow-up questions that build upon the other person's response and encourages them to share more information. For example, if someone says they enjoy hiking, you could ask, "What's your favorite hiking trail?" or "Have you ever hiked in another country?" Leading the conversation is a great way to ensure that you won't easily run out of things to say.

ASKING ABOUT SOMETHING YOU ALREADY TALKED ABOUT

It's also perfectly acceptable to ask about something you have already talked about. This can be a good way to dive deeper into a particular topic or to show that you are genuinely interested in what the other person has to say. Let's say someone mentioned that they recently went on vacation. By asking "What was your favorite part of the trip?" or "Did you have any unexpected experiences while you were there?" we show our interest and uncover common ground to talk about.

BE INTERESTED IN DETAILS

Finally, if you're interested in details, it's important to ask questions that allow the other person to share more information. This could involve asking about their thoughts, feelings, or experiences. Someone might mention that they enjoy cooking. In this situation, we could ask "What's your favorite thing to cook?" or "How did you learn to cook so well?"

ENDING A CONVERSATION GRACEFULLY

During his time as a master's student at the University of Oxford, Adam Mastroianni faced a common fear: getting trapped in a conversation with no polite way out. He then wondered if his conversational partner had the same fear, which led him to conduct a study that led to a shocking conclusion. Most conversations don't end when people want them to (Mastroianni et al., 2021).

The researchers discovered that people hide their true desires to avoid being rude, making it difficult to guess their conversational partner's wishes. This can lead to discomfort and awkwardness for both parties, especially if one person is trying to prolong the conversation while the other is ready to move on. Fortunately, there are ways to end a conversation gracefully and politely.

If you've enjoyed the conversation and would like to see the other person again, you can express this by saying something like, "I've really enjoyed talking with you. Would you be interested in exchanging contact information so we can stay in touch?" This gives the other person an opportunity to accept or decline the offer, depending on their level of interest.

Small talk is often seen as a precursor to more meaningful conversations, so I pay attention to what the other person is saying. This helps me recall the conversation later on and makes the speaker feel heard. That way, the next time we meet, we'll have something to talk about. I can refer back to something they said in our previous conversation. This shows the other person that I've been paying attention and am interested in getting to know them better.

When you're ready to leave, it's helpful to reiterate something that was discussed during the conversation as a way of tying things up neatly. This not only shows that you were engaged in the conversation, but it also gives a clear indication that the conversation is coming to an end.

Sometimes it can be useful to frame the end of the conversation as a slightly regrettable event. This is a way of acknowledging that the conversation was enjoyable but that it's time to move on. It's a great way to smooth over any potential awkwardness or discomfort and leave both parties feeling positive about the interaction.

CHAPTER FIVE KEY TAKEAWAYS

✓ Small talk is a great way to build rapport and connection with others. Mastering the art is an important step to improving our conversational skills.

✓ Small talk topics come in all shapes and sizes, so some topics will make for better conversations while others don't. It is better to steer clear from emotionally charged and highly divisive topics such as politics, finance, or religion. when making small talk.

✓ Silence during a conversation is normal and can signify many things. Fortunately, it is easy enough to deal with awkward silences by asking open-ended and leading questions.

✓ When moving on from small talk and talking about yourself, present yourself in an interesting light. Focus on your strengths and passions instead of only stating the basic facts about where you work and what you like.

✓ Most people want to end a conversation sooner than when we realize, so we need to remain mindful of the other person's feelings and needs.

CHAPTER SIX:

FOUNDATIONS OF GOOD COMMUNICATION

"Take advantage of every opportunity to practice your communication skills so that when important occasions arise, you will have the gift, the style, the sharpness, the clarity, and the emotions to affect other people."

— JIM ROHN —

Effective communication is key to building healthy relationships, both personally and professionally, and involves more than just speaking and being heard. So, what is the secret to effective communication? It took me a while to discover the answer. After a lot of thought on the matter, I concluded that the secret must lie in our actions. Effective communication requires active listening, sincere interest, and a willingness to understand and connect with others.

Active listening is an important communication skill that involves paying close attention to the speaker and making an effort to understand their message. Active listening helps to build trust and rapport between the speaker and the listener. When someone feels heard and understood, they are more likely to open up and share their thoughts and feelings. It also promotes understanding by allowing the listener to gain a deeper insight into the speaker's perspective, thoughts, and feelings. This understanding can help to avoid misunderstandings and miscommunications. Overall, active listening is an essential communication skill that can improve the quality of conversations and relationships.

A study published in the *Proceedings of the National Academy of Sciences* found that people tend to enjoy talking about themselves more than listening to others. The study found that talking about oneself activates the same pleasure centers in the brain as food, money, and sex (Tamir & Mitchell, 2012).

The researchers in this study conducted a series of experiments using functional magnetic resonance imaging (fMRI) to measure brain activity in response to different stimuli, including talking about oneself and listening to others talk about themselves.

The results showed that people experienced a significant increase in activity in the mesolimbic dopamine system, which is associated with reward and pleasure when talking about themselves. This suggests that self-disclosure is inherently pleasurable.

However, the study also found that excessive self-disclosure can have negative effects on social interactions. When one person dominates the conversation and focuses too much on themselves, it can lead others to feel less connected and less engaged. The researchers suggest that balancing self-disclosure with active listening can help improve social interactions and promote more positive feelings between individuals.

Effective communication is not a competition. It's not about who speaks the most or who "wins" the conversation. Instead, it's about creating a space where everyone feels heard, valued, and respected. A little silence after someone has spoken can show respect and allow everyone to process what has been said. It's okay to speak less and listen more, as long as you are engaged and interested in what others are saying. By focusing on others, showing respect, and being true to ourselves, we can create deeper and more meaningful connections with those around us. In this chapter, we'll be covering a lot of different tips and approaches. Not all tips and approaches will work for everyone, so pick the ones that you feel will work for you. It might take some trial and error, but you'll find the approach that works best.

WHAT IT REALLY MEANS TO LISTEN

Not all forms of listening are created equal. Sometimes we only listen to respond and don't really listen to understand. This can have a drastic impact on our communication ability, as a 2015 study found. The study argues that active listening not only helps the listener to better understand the speaker's message but also helps the speaker to communicate more effectively.

The study begins by defining active listening as a communication skill that involves paying close attention to the speaker, asking clarifying questions, and providing feedback to confirm understanding. The authors then review previous research on the benefits of active listening, including improved relationships, reduced conflict, and increased job satisfaction.

The authors then present their own research, which involved a survey of employees from various organizations. The survey asked participants about their use of active listening skills in workplace conversations, as well as their perceptions of their own communication skills and the communication skills of their colleagues. The results showed that employees who reported using active listening skills more frequently also reported higher levels of communication competence and perceived their colleagues to be better communicators. The study draws the conclusion that improving our active listening skills can have a positive impact on communication (Baker & Warren, 2015).

Based on the study's findings we can safely draw the conclusion that most meaningful conversations are based on active listening. Through active listening, we aim to understand what the other person is saying, instead of plastering our own narrative on events. But how exactly does one listen to understand? It is a skill that we'll need to learn and hone, but the tips that follow will help you on the right track.

PAY ATTENTION FULLY

This may be an obvious tip, but it is an important one. Too often people are distracted by their cell phones, the television, or something that's nagging at the back of their minds to give someone their full attention. There are some simple steps we can take to minimize distractions:

- Making eye contact and facing the person you're talking to.

- Don't try to multitask.

- If you find your attention slipping and your thoughts drifting, gently refocus your attention on the present.

- Put the phone and other electronic distractions away.

A handy trick I've learned to help improve concentration is to focus on my breath. Go ahead and try it, the steps are simple. Inhale through the nose and take note of how your ribcage expands and lungs fill as air rushes in. Use your diaphragm to ensure you are taking deep, slow breaths. Exhale slowly through the mouth now. Take note of how it feels when your breath rushes past your lips. Notice any bodily sensations that might arise. Keep your breaths slow and steady as you concentrate on the rhythm. Did you notice how it helped to calm down any racing thoughts and improved concentration? Try it when you have a conversation next and see the difference it makes!

If you find that your thoughts wander to other topics while doing this breathing exercise, gently redirect your attention to your breathing. The idea is to use the breath as a tool to train our concentration. It's similar to the practices we find in yoga and meditation. These disciplines have been proven to reduce stress and anxiety, which is useful not only from a communication perspective but from a general health one, too.

HEAR WHAT THEY HAVE TO SAY

Ever had a conversation with someone who was in the habit of cutting you off, interrupting you, or jumping to conclusions? It can be a frustrating experience that leaves us feeling very unsatisfied with the conversation. Worst of all, it can leave us with the impression that we haven't been heard, which can be pretty hurtful.

When we are in the habit of interrupting people we are not listening to understand, we're simply listening to respond. This does not provide us with a good foundation for communication at all. Keep in mind that interrupting a person while they speak essentially translates into a lack of respect for the other person. It does not create a favorable impression, and this bad habit should be avoided.

REPEAT POINTS FOR CLARITY

An easy way to enhance our understanding of what was said is to repeat a point. If someone mentions that they like candy canes because it's sweet and minty, we can demonstrate our understanding by saying something like "Because they're sweet and minty? Which brand would you recommend?" Other ways we can show our understanding include:

- Paraphrasing what the person said. "It sounds like what you said is..." and "What I'm hearing is..." are common ways to paraphrase and repeat what the individual said.

- By asking questions starting with "What do you mean with..." or "Did you mean that..." we can show our understanding and ask for clarity on something.

- Repeat certain words back to the speaker every once in while during the conversation to show that you are paying attention.

These various forms of repetition and showing our understanding are useful to show to the other person that we are paying attention and listening to what they are saying. The end result is that the person will feel heard, which goes a long way toward establishing rapport and creating meaningful connections!

RESPOND WHEN IT'S YOUR TURN

After we listened closely to what the other person has said and they finished speaking, we'll need to respond. It can be easy to fall into the habit of just going back to what we wanted to say originally, but in doing so we'll risk creating the impression that we never listened to the speaker in the first place!

To prevent this from happening, we'll need to address the key points of what was said for the sake of clarity. It is fine to pause for a few seconds to gather your thoughts, after which we share our thoughts as accurately as possible.

By using these tips you'll notice a difference in the quality of your conversations and how you are being listened to, as well. When we listen to others respectfully, they tend to return the favor!

WHY THE POWER OF PAUSE MATTERS

Pauses can create a natural rhythm and flow in a conversation, allowing us to take a moment to reflect and respond thoughtfully to what people are saying. By mastering the power of pauses, we can improve our communication skills and build stronger connections with others.

One of the benefits of pausing is that it allows us to gather our thoughts before speaking. When we take a moment to think about what we want to say, we can communicate more clearly and effectively. In fact, research shows that taking brief pauses during speech can help speakers better organize their thoughts and communicate more effectively (*Pause,* n.d.).

That's not the only thing pauses are good for. Pauses can also help us create a sense of presence and intention in a conversation. By pausing before speaking, we signal to the other person that we are fully engaged in the conversation and are taking time to consider our response.

Intentional pauses and silences in conversations can help build trust, enhance communication effectiveness, and create a safe space for individuals to share their thoughts and feelings, according to a 2019 study (Vardhman et al., 2019). The study suggests that mastering the power of pauses and silences can significantly improve one's conversational intelligence.

The most obvious benefit of a pause is to create an opportunity for the other person to respond. Some people can talk a mile a minute, making it nearly impossible to get a word in edgewise. When we pause after asking a question or sharing a thought, we give the other person time to consider their response and share their perspective. This can lead to more thoughtful and meaningful conversations where both parties feel heard and understood.

It's important to note that pauses can also be used strategically to influence the outcome of a conversation. For example, pausing after making a request can create a sense of expectation and encourage the other person to comply with our request. Use this technique ethically so that others are not manipulated or coerced.

By taking the time to pause and reflect, we can improve our communication skills and build stronger connections with others. So, the next time you find yourself in a conversation, remember to take a breath and use the power of pauses to your advantage.

USING THE POWER OF QUESTIONS

I find that asking questions is a great way to build a connection with someone and get to know them better. But there are different types of questions that we can ask, and it's important to understand when and for what purpose to use them. There are five types of questions we use in everyday conversations, so we'll take a closer look at these.

OPEN-ENDED QUESTIONS
These are good questions to have in your conversational arsenal. These questions are perfect to

get extra information, overcome awkward silences, and build rapport. All of this is made possible because we can't answer these questions with a simple "yes" or "no." All those "who," "where," "when," "why," "what," and "how" questions encourage us to give longer answers, which helps keep the conversation alive.

Just a word of caution on using "why" questions is needed here, as these questions tend to make people defensive. When we ask a "why" question, it can come across that we are questioning a person's actions and want them to justify themselves. As you can imagine, this does not encourage people to answer and keep the conversation going.

CLOSED-ENDED QUESTIONS
These are questions that typically have a limited set of response options, often requiring a simple "yes" or "no" answer. Examples include, "Did you enjoy the movie?" or "Have you ever been to Paris?" They're great to narrow down our options, but horrible at keeping a conversation going. Use these questions sparingly to keep the conversation flowing.

PROBING QUESTIONS
These questions show that we are interested in a topic and want to know more. They are often used to follow up on an answer to an open-ended question. Examples include "Can you explain what you meant by that?" or "Could you give me an example?" These questions are a good choice to build rapport, uncover common ground, and foster understanding.

LEADING QUESTIONS

These are questions that suggest or imply a particular answer, often influencing the person to respond in a certain way. Examples include, "Don't you think that's a bad idea?" or "Wouldn't you agree that X is the best choice?"

Leading questions should be used with discretion as they can be seen as manipulative. By structuring our questions a certain way, we are creating an expectation that the person answering should agree with us. As you can imagine, leading questions won't help us understand what other people think or feel about Product X or that new film everyone's been raving about. We'll need to ask open-ended questions to create this understanding and uncover common ground.

HYPOTHETICAL QUESTIONS

These are questions that ask what could or would happen in a particular situation. They are often used to explore possibilities or test someone's reasoning or decision-making skills. Examples include "What would you do if you won the lottery?" or "How would you handle a difficult customer?" These questions are good to use when we're getting to know somebody and building rapport.

MAKING QUESTIONS LESS INTRUSIVE

Sometimes when we ask questions they may come across as interrogative. To prevent this unfortunate situation from happening, we need to make our questions more conversational. To do this, we need to soften our language.

I'll explain this with the help of an example. I could ask my favorite author, "What is your biggest success story?" While there is technically nothing wrong with this question, it certainly won't inspire the author to answer it, either. It is a little too direct. A good way to soften this question would be: "I'd love to understand your journey as an author; what is your biggest success story?" By softening the question, I not only asked the author to provide me with context for their answer but also gave them a reason why I asked the question.

Another way we can soften our questions is by making use of presuppositions. If I were to soften my question to the author even further using a preposition, it would look something like this: "I'd love to understand your journey as an author; would you be able to share with me what your biggest success story was?"

By softening our language and using prepositions, we can make questions sound less like an interrogation and more like a conversation! Give it a try in your next conversation and experience the difference it can make. You'll likely find that people will be more willing to answer softened questions, which helps keep the conversation going.

However, there are also mistakes to avoid when asking questions. Sometimes, when people ask a question, they'll include long statements to try and soften their language. The question ends up being very wordy and unclear. One way to prevent misunderstandings when dealing with wordy questions is to summarize the content and ask for clarity. A simple "Just to check my understanding, are you asking about...." is sufficient. We're using a closed-ended question to check our understanding so that we can give the person the information they are asking for.

Another common mistake people often make is to ask questions that are too personal or intrusive. This can make the other person uncomfortable. Examples of intrusive questions include:

- Why are you still single?

- Did you have a difficult childhood?

- Have you ever been arrested?

- Do you have any mental health issues?

It is important to be mindful of the questions we ask others and to respect their boundaries and privacy. Asking intrusive questions can damage relationships and make people feel uncomfortable or embarrassed.

Using loops is another great way to continue a conversation and build rapport. If a topic has been discussed previously, you can always come back to it later in the conversation to keep the discussion going. So, by harnessing the power of questions in a positive way, we can create deeper and more meaningful conversations with the people around us.

HARNESSING THE POWER OF STORIES

The art of storytelling is an ancient and enduring tradition that has served as a means of communication and entertainment for millennia. Even if you feel your life is unremarkable, it is possible to find compelling stories within your experiences. Having a few good anecdotes to hand when they are needed can be helpful. Building a "story bank" with tales about work, hobbies, local events, and personal achievements can be an excellent way to ensure that you are always ready to entertain or inform.

Anything can be transformed into a good story when told with enthusiasm, but to help you along, here are some questions that can help you find a suitable story to tell.

- Do you like entertaining stories about pets and animals?

- Do you like action-packed stories or wholesome tales?

- Do you like serious or informative stories?

- Do stories on current affairs tickle your fancy, or are cute, lovey-dovey stories more your speed?

No matter what story you like, keep in mind that a good story has something relatable in it. Now that we know how to find a story, we only need to figure out how to tell a good story. Fortunately, the tips below will help you with that!

KEEP IT SHORT AND USE BOLD ADJECTIVES

To tell a good story, it is essential to engage your audience and keep them interested. One way to do this is to use bold, exciting adjectives to describe your story. This will pique the listener's curiosity and make them more likely to want to hear more. It is also important to keep the story brief and to the point. A good short story has a clear action, a brief summary, and one emotion. This combination provides the listener with enough information to understand the story while keeping it concise and easy to remember.

CREATE THE MOOD

When telling a story, creating the right atmosphere is crucial. Your tone of voice and body language can significantly influence how your story is received. By making eye contact, using hand gestures, and projecting your voice, you can make your storytelling more engaging and dynamic. It's also essential to express your emotions and feelings in the story. This connection with the audience can create a more captivating experience.

LEAVE THEM CRAVING MORE

It is essential to leave the audience wanting more. One way to achieve this is by allowing them to imagine the events of the story before they dive into the details. By using open-ended questions, you can encourage your listeners to guess what happened, thus making them more invested in the story. It's also important to avoid using jargon or technical language that the listener may not understand, as this can lead to confusion and disinterest. Here's an example for inspiration:

"I met my cat in the weirdest way! I came home from work and heard the scariest sound coming from my kitchen! What would you have done? Well, I grabbed a broom and snuck to the kitchen, expecting an intruder. Instead, I found a cat with a litter of kittens!"

STAY AWAY FROM JARGON

If your audience doesn't understand what you are saying, they will lose interest and stop listening. This is why it is extra important to avoid jargon. Focus on telling your story using simple, easy-to-understand words. Try to avoid using complex terms to explain your story to a listener; simply tell them why the story is important and make it relatable (like we did with our cat story).

Keep in mind that storytelling takes practice, but if you stay relevant to your audience and keep the tips we discussed in mind, chances are you'll be well on your way to becoming a great storyteller.

TYPES OF STORIES

There are various ways to narrate a story, but for our intention, we will briefly focus on three story types that effortlessly captivate audiences. These are listener stories, connection stories, and stories with shock value. It's important to note that all stories follow the classic structure of having a beginning, middle, and end, and usually involve overcoming a challenge. With that in mind, let's delve deeper into the types of stories we can utilize to convey our message effectively.

LISTENER STORIES

Here, the storyteller does most of the talking while the audience mainly listens. This type of story is commonly used in motivational speeches and sales pitches, where the storyteller describes what the audience has experienced or is currently going through. Listener stories can be incredibly powerful and persuasive, especially when we highlight common experiences that people may have had. These kinds of stories are a good way to build rapport.

CONNECTION STORIES

These stories can be divided into two categories: personal connection stories and stories about other people. When sharing personal connection stories, it's crucial to help the audience identify with the story. These stories are similar to listener stories, but the crucial difference is that the story is about the storyteller. Social media influencers often use stories about other people to create rapport and encourage people to take action without directly telling them what to do. The trick is to allow the audience to come to their conclusions.

STORIES WITH SHOCK VALUE

These stories are useful for getting people thinking and can be a useful strategy to quell any objections that may arise. These stories often involve a surprise element that causes the audience to question their assumptions or perspective. While the ethics of using this tactic can be questionable, it can be an effective strategy to convey a message.

ADDING SPICE TO STORIES

Now that we've got the different kinds of stories down pat, we can look at ways to liven up our storytelling. Metaphors and analogies can be powerful tools for storytelling, as they help to create vivid imagery and make abstract concepts more concrete and relatable to the reader or listener. Here are some tips on how to use metaphors and analogies effectively in your storytelling:

- UNDERSTAND THE CONCEPT YOU WANT TO CONVEY: To use a metaphor or analogy, you must first understand the concept you want to convey. Take time to reflect on the idea you want to express and think about the images, symbols, or situations that might best illustrate it.

- USE FAMILIAR OBJECTS OR EXPERIENCES: To make your metaphors and analogies relatable to your audience, try to use familiar objects or experiences that they can easily relate to. For example, if you are trying to describe a complicated process, you might compare it to assembling a jigsaw puzzle.

- BE CREATIVE AND ORIGINAL: While it's important to use familiar objects or experiences, you should also try to be creative and original with your metaphors and analogies. A fresh or unexpected comparison can grab your audience's attention and make your story more memorable.

- AVOID MIXED METAPHORS: Mixing metaphors can be confusing and undermine your credibility as a storyteller. Stick to one clear comparison throughout your story.

- USE SENSORY LANGUAGE: When using a metaphor or analogy, try to use sensory language to help your audience vividly imagine the comparison you are making. For example, instead of saying "She was as cold as ice," you might say "Her words cut through me like a knife."

Overall, the key to using metaphors and analogies effectively is to be thoughtful, creative, and clear in your storytelling. With practice, you can develop your ability to use these powerful tools to engage your audience and make your stories more compelling.

How to Communicate in Group Settings

Our ability to adapt to different contexts and communication styles and our understanding of group dynamics influence how effectively we'll communicate in a group setting. Whether you're delivering a presentation on packaging materials or having a high-stakes team meeting, communicating in group settings has its own special challenges. Fortunately, there are several strategies that we can use to improve our communication skills in these situations.

Prepare in Advance
One way we can feel more comfortable communicating in a group is to prepare in advance. This means taking time to think through what we want to say and practicing our delivery. By preparing in advance, we can feel more confident and prepared to participate in group conversations. For many people, it's easier to tweak something if they can see what they are doing. This is where a mirror comes in handy. By practicing different delivery styles in front of the mirror, we can have the double benefit of seeing what the delivery looks like, giving us a better idea of how and where to refine it.

Find Common Ground

Sometimes we may feel more comfortable communicating in a group when we can find common ground with other members. This is why people tend to talk about golf and food at business meetings. These topics tend to be shared experiences, giving other members of the group something to relate to. By finding common ground, we can build connections with members and feel more comfortable participating in group conversations.

Speak up When You Have Something to Say

Do you feel hesitant to speak up in a group setting? This happens to everyone from time to time, but it is important to share your thoughts and ideas when you have something to say.

To do this, consider using nonverbal cues to indicate that you want to speak, such as raising your hand, clearing your throat, nodding your head, or speaking up when there is a pause in the conversation. By speaking up when we have something to say, we can contribute to the group's conversation and share valuable insights.

Take a Break if You Need It

Group conversations can be overwhelming at times, especially when there are many people speaking at once. When group conversations become overwhelming we may benefit from taking breaks when needed to recharge and regroup. This could involve stepping outside for a few minutes or taking a few deep breaths. By taking breaks when needed, we'll feel more energized and engaged when we return to the group.

These strategies can help us feel more comfortable and confident communicating in a group. Keep in mind that it will take some patience and practice, but it is possible for everyone to have fulfilling and engaging group conversations.

COMMON COMMUNICATION MISTAKES TO AVOID

Even the best communicators make mistakes. These mistakes can easily lead to misunderstandings, conflicts, and potentially damage relationships. There is good news though, as many of these potential conflicts and misunderstandings can be prevented if we strive to avoid these common mistakes.

SAYING "YES, BUT"

One common mistake is to use "yes, but" instead of "yes, and" when communicating with others. I found that it was one of the smallest changes that I needed to make, but it had the biggest impact on my quality of communication.

"Yes, but" is often used to disagree with or dismiss the other person's ideas, while "yes, and" encourages collaboration and builds upon the other person's ideas (Hopkins, 2020). By using "yes, and" we can create a positive and open-minded environment for communication and ensure that everyone's ideas are heard. Try it the next time you have a conversation and experience the difference it makes!

FOCUSSING ON FIXED IDEAS

Another mistake is to focus on fixed ideas and opinions rather than the flow of communication. This can lead to a closed-minded approach and prevent you from considering alternative perspectives (Doyle, 2021). Instead, try to be open-minded and flexible, and focus on understanding the other person's point of view.

AVOID NEGATIVITY

Negativity can easily creep into a conversation, but it is another mistake we should avoid. Negative comments and criticism can be hurtful and demotivating and can damage relationships. Instead, try to provide constructive feedback and focus on solutions rather than problems (Goldsmith, n.d.).

DON'T SPEAK POORLY ABOUT OTHERS

It's also important to avoid talking negatively about others, especially when you don't know them well. This can create a negative impression and damage your own reputation (Riegel, 2018). If someone asks for your opinion on someone else, you can respond that you don't know them well enough to provide a meaningful comment. By doing this you draw a clear boundary that you are not willing to engage in the topic, while being respectful towards the people around you.

AVOID SHOWING OFF YOUR IQ

Lastly, don't try to show that you are the smartest person in the room. Some people do this, mistakenly believing it makes them appear more interesting or likable to other people. In reality, showing off how clever you are can create a competitive and confrontational environment and prevent effective communication. Instead, focus on listening actively and contributing constructively to the conversation (Baldoni, 2014). There are other ways of becoming more charismatic, interesting, and likable to the people around you, but we'll discuss that in the next chapter.

CHAPTER SIX KEY TAKEAWAYS

✓ Active listening is an important skill that helps to build trust and rapport between the speaker and the listener. When someone feels heard and understood, they are more likely to open up and share their thoughts and feelings.

✓ Questions are a great way to get to know someone, but we need to use them carefully. Closed-ended questions can shut a conversation down while open-ended questions encourage a conversation to flow.

✓ There's no need to fill every waking moment with speech. Pauses have a place in conversations and can add meaning to what is being said.

✓ Storytelling is a powerful medium to get our ideas across and capture the listener's attention! Keep in mind that effective stories are short, use bold adjectives, and leave the listener craving more details.

✓ There are different types of stories we can tell to get our point across. Connection stories, listener stories, and stories with shock value are great ways to spice up our communication and command the attention of the listener. Anything can be turned into a story with a little bit of thought.

✓ Metaphors and analogies are great tools to use to add spice and variety to stories.

✓ It is possible for everyone to communicate effectively when they find themselves in a group setting. By finding common ground and mustering the courage to speak up when they have something to say, everyone can contribute meaningfully to group conversations.

✓ Common communication mistakes, such as focusing on fixed ideas and speaking poorly of others, can place a wrench in the spokes of communication. It is best to avoid these mistakes wherever possible and focus on honing constructive communication skills (like those discussed in the previous chapters).

CHAPTER SEVEN:

BECOMING THE BEST VERSION OF YOU

"Pursuing your passions makes you more interesting, and interesting people are enchanting."

— GUY KAWASAKI —

When I think of charisma, I think of people who have a presence. You know, those people who walk into a room and captivate everyone when they speak. It's an experience being around charismatic people, and they have the ability to sway our opinions. A 2003 study examined the relationship between charisma and trustworthiness, as well as the ability to influence the attitudes and opinions of others.

In this study, participants were asked to rate the charisma of a hypothetical leader based on a set of personality traits and behaviors. The study found that individuals who were perceived as more charismatic were also rated as more trustworthy by the participants.

Additionally, these individuals were found to be more effective at influencing the attitudes and opinions of others. This suggests that charisma may play an important role in establishing trust and credibility with others, which in turn can increase one's ability to influence them (Jost et al., 2004).

While the study focused on a hypothetical scenario, the findings suggest that charisma can have important implications for interpersonal communication. While it may seem that some individuals are blessed with ample amounts of personal charm, many behavioral scientists hold firm that it is a learned behavior.

Charisma essentially boils down to your emotional approachability and your ability to motivate (*Can You Learn How to Be Charismatic,* 2020). Charismatic people have a way of managing their nerves and being confident. They believe that they are supposed to be a part of the interactions they're in, and they don't put too much pressure on themselves or the outcome of the situation.

Everything you've been learning in this book so far has been preparing you for this. That's right! You are ready for this. In social situations, try to focus on enjoying the moment; that way, your natural charm will shine through. As we had a lot of tips in previous chapters, you can expect that in this chapter we'll discuss different tips and approaches too. Simply select the tips and approaches that you feel will work the best for you.

We might think that charm is about saying the right things, having a cool catchphrase, or dazzling others with our bright insights. In reality, we don't need to be entertainers or politicians to be charismatic. Charisma, like every human being, is a beautifully unique thing. We only need to listen, be curious, and be warm and open for our natural charm to shine through.

BECOMING AN INTERESTING PERSON

In the last chapter, we spoke about how our storytelling skills can be improved to make us sound more interesting. While it is true that a good storyteller can make brewing a cup of coffee into an exciting tale, we need to be proactive and cultivate habits that add value to our lives.

All too often, we find ourselves stuck in the rut of going to work, coming home, and binge-watching series or playing video games. There's nothing wrong with living a simple life, but we are not exposing ourselves to new experiences when we become so entrenched in our habits.

Much like a vehicle that is stuck in the mud, our value-detracting habits prevent us from seeing new places and doing new things. I'm not saying you need to change everything you do! Not at all. There's comfort in familiarity. What I am suggesting is that when you feel ready to take your communication skills to the next level, spice things up in your life by applying these tips. Your social life will thank you.

READ MORE

Reading is probably the only way people can install new software in their brains. It is an amazing pastime that enriches our lives by opening the door to fictional worlds and fascinating theories. Many popular films, series, and games were originally books, so reading is still a very relevant pastime in our world of snappy dance videos and quirky photo filters. As an added bonus, reading can enhance our concentration skills, plus it is a great stress reliever (*Reading Improves Memory, Concentration and Stress,* 2016).

Starting a reading habit is not complicated. Simply find a book in the genre that you love, and books you wouldn't normally read, as well. Don't like books? Try reading news articles, magazines, comics, or manga.

When we start looking, we'll find many things to read! If you're an avid gamer try reading the in-game lore instead of clicking hastily past it to continue slaying monsters. When I developed my reading habit, I found that the more I read the more curious I became about the world around me. Perhaps you'll experience the same.

SWITCH THINGS UP

Another way to make life more interesting is to vary your routine. While there may be comfort in familiarity, it is important to break the monotony of daily life. It makes for great conversations!

You don't have to do anything crazy but embrace doing things just because you feel like it. You'll never know what experiences you are going to have! I remember going for a walk with my dogs by the river when I saw an eagle feeding peacefully on a branch. The eagle was devouring a fish, and I was so close I could see its talons dig into the branch. Watching that eagle feed was a magical moment that I would have missed if I stuck to my routine of work, home, and sleep!

VOLUNTEER

Not only is volunteering a great way to make our lives more interesting, but it is beneficial for everyone involved. In exchange for helping other people and communities, we gain unique experiences that help make our lives interesting. In the laws of alchemy, according to popular television tropes, that's equivalent to exchange!

Embrace Different Views

Change can be scary, so here's an actionable tip most of us can try right now. Whenever we try something new and get that all-too-familiar knot in our stomachs, try to step through it. While small talk is an important first step to getting a conversation started, it is not enough to sustain a conversation, and it certainly won't deliver new viewpoints to us. After everything we've learned in this book so far, you come too far to take the easy way out. So instead of asking the same old questions regarding someone's work or personal life, try asking them what's on their bucket list or the weirdest thing they've eaten. Give your questions a fresh approach. Who knows? The answers to your questions might lead to new insights. In the next chapter, we'll look at ways to deepen the conversation.

There are many ways we can be proactive and create interesting lives for ourselves. In doing so we'll have more to talk about and generate more opportunities to create conversations with interesting people. Sure, we may need to overcome some value-detracting habits, but if we take it one step at a time, it can be done.

Nurture Conversational Intelligence

Another aspect of becoming interesting, charismatic, and likable is our conversational intelligence. All too often people may find themselves trapped in a conversation that they do not enjoy. The person they are conversing with might be under the impression that they are charming and interesting, even if the other person thinks otherwise.

Now imagine if the shoe was on the other foot and we are the ones blissfully unaware of our lacking conversational intelligence. That would make it difficult to connect with people, that's for sure. It can take some discipline, practice, and self-awareness to stop treating conversations as a monologue, but there is one thing we can do to prevent this: don't assume.

People tend to make assumptions, but these are dangerous things to make as they often leave us in trouble. Whether we assume we know what others think, or that the meaning of our words is clear, assumptions can lead us down the path of alienation if we're not careful.

When we leave our assumptions at the door, ask questions, and show genuine interest in the conversation, we develop conversational intelligence. This skill can be defined as our ability to understand others and have conversations with them, and how these conversations influence those around us. Everything you've learned so far is geared toward developing conversational intelligence, so don't sweat it. Keep practicing and you'll do great.

OVERCOMING THE "BORING" TRAP

Although many people try to be interesting, there are still many individuals who are considered boring despite their best efforts. A study led by a researcher from the University of Essex aimed to identify the most stereotypical boring jobs, hobbies, and characteristics, and investigated the negative impact of being perceived as boring. The study results showed that accounting, tax/insurance, cleaning, banking, sleeping, religion, watching TV, observing animals, and doing math were considered the most boring jobs and hobbies.

Meanwhile, stereotypical bores were described as having no interests, no sense of humor, being unopinionated, or being a bit of a complainer. Moreover, the study revealed that being perceived as boring had substantially negative interpersonal consequences, affecting perceptions of warmth and competence, and resulting in social avoidance (van Tilburg et al., 2022).

From the study results, we can draw a conclusion that a lack of fun definitely contributes to the perception of being boring. The big question now is, how can we avoid being labeled as uninteresting people? These tips should help:

- Communication is more about fun. Think about it as a game. Enjoy yourself. Laugh at yourself. Be relaxed, open, warm, and playful.

- You can select and change hobbies and traits you share with others and how you describe them.

- Try different conversation starters that get people thinking. Ask people what the best part of their week was, what motivates them to get up in the morning, or if they have any passions they are pursuing at the moment. These questions will draw out emotions and can result in the most unique and memorable conversations.

BECOMING MORE CAPTIVATING

In the previous chapter, we spoke about why the power of pauses matters. What I did not mention is that pauses can also be used to command people's full attention. The only challenge here is that the pause needs to be long enough to achieve this.

There's a super easy way to practice this. All you need to do is record your voice while talking about anything and insert a pause. Play the recording, and if you can hardly detect the pause in speech, it was not long enough.

To hold a person's attention, the pause needs to be long enough to be slightly uncomfortable. This is a great technique to get people's attention if you are giving a speech or delivering a presentation. Correctly using pauses is one of the many ways we can become more captivating.

REFRAIN FROM USING FILLER WORDS

Next time you hear a confident person speak, listen closely to the way they use their voice and language.

Chances are, their voice is confident, relaxed, and with a tone that dips down at the end of each sentence.

Most importantly, you'll be able to detect very few "ums" and "ahs." One of the biggest signs that we are nervous is the use of filler words such as "um," "ah," and "eh." Thankfully, it is very easy to address this issue. Whenever you feel the need to use a filler word, slow down and pause. It will take a bit of practice, but soon enough you'll be able to rid your speech of these unwanted words.

READ AND USE BASIC BODY LANGUAGE

Next time you're watching a public or motivational speaker, take note of their breathing. When we maintain a slow and steady breath, we appear more confident. This is because doing so reduces our stress levels (Thompson, 2017).

Taking relaxed, deep breaths while we are speaking also helps our voices to project better. This creates a stronger image of confidence. Confidence is a wonderful thing to nurture because it makes it more likely that people will find you interesting (Van Edwards, n.d.).

One way we can ensure to appear more confident is by consciously adopting the body language that is associated with confidence, such as taking relaxed deep breaths, making eye contact, and adopting a straight posture.

We can use body language to show people that we are listening simply by nodding our heads from time to time. This shows that we agree with what the person is saying and that we are listening.

ANALOG MARKING FOR PERSUASIVENESS

Listen to any motivational or public speaker. Chances are, they have this advanced technique down pat. Analog marking is a method we can use to highlight certain parts of what we are saying by using our voices and bodies. An example will illustrate this point well.

"When shopping for food items low in salt, it is important that we remember to..." (Pause) "read the label!" (Command tone).

See what we did there? A pause helped us get everyone's attention before we delivered the main point of what we wanted to say in a strong command tone. That is analog marking.

We can combine analog marking with body language and use our hands to indicate a reading gesture to punctuate the message even more. If analog marking seems a bit too complex for you at the moment, don't stress too much about it. Effective communication can still take place without it.

GET PASSIONATE

Our voices are capable of conveying a range of emotions. Voice actors have mastered the art of adding expression to their voices and breathing life into their words. You can do this, too, with a little practice and the help of your cell phone. Simply record yourself saying something in your normal tone of voice. Now repeat what you said, but this time add expression to it. Play back the recording and notice the difference between the two deliveries. If you can hardly tell the difference between your normal tone of voice and the expressive one, you'll need to exaggerate what you are saying to produce a noticeable effect.

Another great way to practice adding expression to your voice is to read a story out loud. Try to bring the story to life with your voice, just like a voice actor would. In time, you'll notice that adding expression to your voice will become more natural as you practice and get used to using your voice in this way.

CONTROL YOUR TONE

When speaking, pay attention to how your voice rises and falls. When our voices rise at the end of a sentence, it can indicate a question or uncertainty. If our voices constantly rise at the end of sentences, it can be hard for other people to take us seriously when it matters.

Let's say an object sailed through the air and you needed to duck. If someone shouted "Get down!" with a rising tone of voice, it would be confusing and could easily be interpreted as a question. However, if that same person shouted "Get down!" in a commanding voice (where the tone goes down at the end of a sentence), it would be easily understood. How you say something truly matters.

SOUNDING WELL-READ

Think of people that you consider great communicators. Chances are, these people have an outstanding command of English. But excellent communicators have another thing in common: They know when to use their extended vocabulary and when to use everyday words.

These individuals create the impression of being well-read and sounding intelligent without overwhelming the listener with their impressive vocabulary or sounding pompous. How do they do it? Well, the trick is quite simple, but you need to select your audience carefully.

If you are having a conversation with someone who has a limited vocabulary, it is best to stick to everyday words. When we are speaking with someone with an extended vocabulary, we can slip in one or two lesser-known words in the conversation to gain credibility.

It should go without saying that these words should be used appropriately; otherwise, we'll damage our credibility. So, it is always a good idea to check the meaning of words before incorporating them into our vocabulary.

Becoming likable is quite easy. One can be a better listener, offer support, follow up on conversations, find common ground, use positive body language, avoid over-complaining, avoid dominating conversations or bragging, and minimize disagreement—in a nutshell, everything we cover in this book.

However, it is not possible to appeal to all people all of the time, and some individuals may never warm up to someone, even if they are likable. Just focus on being your authentic self and you'll find yourself becoming more likable and charismatic naturally.

Chapter Seven Key Takeaways

✓ Anyone can be charismatic! It is about being confident, warm, and approachable.

✓ To become more interesting as a person, shake up your routine and try something new. Bust out of the "boring" trap and discover a world of experiences and stories just waiting to be told!

✓ Conversational intelligence is another important aspect of becoming interesting, charismatic, and likable. When we stop making assumptions and don't treat conversations as a monologue, we are nurturing this skill.

✓ There are many ways we can use our voices and bodies to become more captivating when we speak. Monitoring our tone of voice, avoiding the use of filler words, and using our voices expressively are some of the ways we can go about this.

CHAPTER EIGHT:

GOING DEEPER IN COMMUNICATION

" Choose to have a conversation with people, rather than talking to people."

— D.J. KYOS —

Research from the American Psychological Association (APA) shows that many people tend to shy away from deep conversations with strangers due to a fear of awkwardness or vulnerability. Instead, they tend to stick to small talk, which is perceived as less risky and less likely to result in discomfort or embarrassment.

While making small talk is an important skill to master, as we discussed in Chapter Five, the findings of the study suggest that there is a benefit to engaging in deep conversations with people. Yet we often overestimate the awkwardness of deep conversations and underestimate the potential for joy and connection that can come from them. After 12 experiments with over 1,800 participants, researchers found that participants reported greater feelings of connection and enjoyment during deep conversations, even though they had initially anticipated that they would be more awkward than they were (Kardas et al., 2021). These findings suggest that deep conversations can bring us a lot of joy, even when we have them with strangers.

Deep conversations help us get to know other people better, so how do we move the conversation into deeper territory? Usually, we have a goal when speaking with others. Whether it is to make friends, nurture networking opportunities, or spark the romantic interest of someone special, our communication skills need to be on point to develop the deep and meaningful connections that we crave. In this chapter, we'll explore how to create and sustain these meaningful connections.

EMPATHETIC COMMUNICATION

Communicating with empathy is a prerequisite for establishing positive and deep relationships. That's because it creates a safe environment for people to open up—a judgment-free zone that encourages others to share more of themselves with us. These conversations leave us feeling good about the encounter as well as more connected to the other person. These are the conversations that we want to nurture.

Have you ever had a conversation with a person who constantly interrupted you before you could finish your thought? It's frustrating, isn't it? Perhaps it felt like this person's mind was elsewhere, or maybe they were quick to dole out advice without fully understanding your thought processes.

How did the interaction make you feel? In most cases, interactions like this leave us uncomfortable and unwilling to share our thoughts with that person in the future. This is because the lack of empathy displayed during the conversation left us feeling that what we had to say carried no value.

Being empathetic does more than create a safe space for communication; it increases our likeability. As we discussed in the previous chapter, embracing different views is essential to sustaining a conversation. But what exactly does it mean to be empathetic?

Empathy can easily be explained when we compare it to sympathy, an emotion it is often confused for. The degree of empathy we possess is reflected in our ability to show compassion toward others and to comprehend them. Sympathy, on the other hand, is more akin to feeling sorry for someone. If pity is our relief at not experiencing a person's issues, then empathy is our capacity to comprehend how they feel (*The Difference between Empathy and Sympathy*, 2022).

Empathy goes further than simply telling another person you understand what they are going through. A person with empathy does not make assumptions, but instead endeavors to understand what the other person is saying, from their perspective. This example should drive the point home. Tobi and Claire had an argument about household chores. Claire raised the point that Tobi rarely helps with chores, to which Tobi responded, "Fine, then. I'll mop and do the laundry this weekend." This response only caused the argument to flare up because it showed zero understanding of Claire's feelings. It lacked empathy. An empathetic response would have sounded something like this:

"It sounds like you feel unappreciated. I haven't been pulling my weight around here, leaving you to do all the chores alone."

This response shows that Tobi is making an effort to try and understand Claire's feelings. Had Tobi responded more empathetically, chances are the argument would never have escalated in the first place.

Empathy is a skill that we can master through active listening, a topic that we've touched on in previous chapters. When we practice empathy, we create an environment that encourages open and trusting relationships and helps us build rapport with others.

BUILDING RAPPORT

To take a conversation to the next level we need to be willing to share our authentic selves with others. In Chapter Two, we spoke about the masks that people wear and learned that through mutual self-disclosure, that mask can be removed.

Mutual self-disclosure happens when two people share things about themselves in a conversation. In the early stages of a relationship or friendship, people are reluctant to share things about themselves, but as the connection deepens, they gradually open up and share more personal details. But how does one go from talking about what you did last week to discussing future plans or sharing deeply-buried hopes? The answer is one step at a time.

We need to remember that a conversation is like climbing the stairs in a multi-story building. As the connection between us and the other person grows and deepens, we move up from the ground floor to find new floors. Each new floor reveals more about the person we're conversing with. I'll explain the levels of self-disclosure like this:

- GROUND FLOOR: On this level, we share facts about ourselves and engage in safe small talk topics. Topics such as owning a pet, having siblings, or what we do for fun or work are typically discussed on this level.

- FIRST FLOOR: The connection between you and the other person is deepened to the extent that you feel safe to share your opinions and beliefs. When we reach this level, we typically disclose our political views, our opinions on current affairs, and our religious background.

- SECOND FLOOR: Continuing upward in the building of communication, when we reach this floor we typically know the person well enough to share our hopes and dreams. Topics such as our career aspirations, whether we'd like to have children or marry, or where we'd like to live are usually discussed on this floor.

- THIRD FLOOR: When we've reached the highest floor in the building of communication, we feel safe enough to share very personal information, such as our insecurities and strange habits.

What floor of the communication building are you on? It is normal to remain on the same floor for quite some time, but there are ways we can ascend the stairs to the next floor a bit more quickly.

After we've determined what floor we're on, we need to set a goal to share more about ourselves with the person we want to nurture a deeper connection. Let's say you're currently on the ground floor with someone, but you'd like to deepen the connection to reach the first floor. Next time you meet, try to share some facts about yourself and observe their reaction. If the person responds positively—if they are curious, interested, or sharing information about themselves, too—it is a good sign.

The following time you meet, you can inch up the stairs to the first floor by sharing your opinions on current affairs, for example. If the response is positive, you can continue to inch up the stairs until you've reached the first floor fully.

Try not to overshare while doing this, as this can leave one feeling vulnerable. Remember, building rapport is like climbing stairs: Take it one step at a time! With a little practice and patience, we'll gain the skills needed to confidently participate in conversations and build rapport at a comfortable pace.

HAVING DEEP CONVERSATIONS

A brief moment of vulnerability has the power to change a conversation entirely. It creates more connections and can elevate a conversation from the shallows to deep, thought-provoking topics. While it may not feel natural to open up to other people at first, you may be pleasantly surprised at how receptive others can be if you do so confidently and calmly.

When deepening the conversation, we need to keep in mind that the conversation is not about a list of psychological problems and family dramas, but about the real you. So it goes without saying that there are some faux pas in deep conversations we need to avoid.

- IT'S NOT A STAGE TO COMPLAIN: Moving on from small talk into deeper topics is about being honest about the less pleasant aspects of life, but it does not give us a stage to complain about our problems.

- ASSUMING THE CONVERSATION WON'T GO DEEPER: A mistake we often make is assuming that other people don't want to move beyond the small talk phase. This assumption will only get in the way of meaningful conversations.

- STEER CLEAR OF EMOTIONALLY CHARGED TOPICS: These topics can be highly divisive, and delving into political, religious, or other divisive topics simply to get a rise out of someone will leave a lasting unfavorable impression.

When deepening the conversation, we should bear in mind that a little goes a long way, or we'll risk coming across as "intense" or "heavy." So don't hesitate to add a little levity to balance out touching moments.

As for secrets, if you feel comfortable enough to share something personal with someone, don't demand that they reciprocate with a secret of their own. This can come across as manipulative and intrusive. Just be honest about the secret you are sharing without creating expectations for a particular response; doing so will only make the conversation awkward.

Sharing shows others that you are real and present. It gives people something to remember you by. However, we need to remain cognizant of the fact that oversharing increases our chances of being judged and disliked, especially when we overshare with strangers. There will always be universally appealing topics that you can talk about with people, but we need to pay attention to the emotional intensity with which we are engaging the topic.

The best advice I can give is that if you want to be friends with someone, treat them as a friend from the start. Share your emotions and build a connection.

We may even make use of mirroring to strengthen a connection with someone. Mirroring (also called "pacing" and "leading" in psychology) happens when we imitate a person we are trying to persuade (Mendonsa, 2018). Many people use this technique without having been taught it. The technique works by mimicking the person you are trying to build a connection with and lead. Things like posture, speech, emotions, and gestures can be copied to build rapport.

This technique should be used with discretion and should never be used for manipulative purposes, as the person you are connecting to in this manner is more likely to view you as a leadership figure. Sales reps use this technique all the time to clinch a deal; this is why they can be so persuasive at times!

Just like there are different stories or levels for building rapport, there are different levels for disclosure. These levels depend entirely on the foundation of trust that has been built. It's only natural to share more about yourself as you get to know someone.

While these levels of disclosure help to create friendships and intimacy, we should bear in mind that it is not needed to reveal everything to everyone. Everyone has secrets they want to keep and it is better not to overshare.

Most importantly, know that people are different and that you don't need everyone you come across to like you. Take the time you need to find your people—the ones that you like and can comfortably communicate with. It will take some practice and effort, but don't give up! You'll find them. In the search for your people, you may come across difficult individuals and situations, but we'll discuss this in the next chapter.

Chapter Eight Key Takeaways

✓ Deep conversations have the potential to bring us a lot of joy, but many people shy away from them due to a fear of awkwardness or vulnerability.

✓ Communicating with empathy is a requirement to get people to open up. Empathy creates a judgment-free zone that lets people feel safe to be a little more vulnerable around us.

✓ Building rapport with people is like ascending the stairs of a multi-story building. We need to take it slowly and one step at a time!

✓ There are different levels for disclosure which we naturally progress through as we get to know someone. These levels depend entirely on the foundation of trust that has been built, so we need to be wary of oversharing as it can hamper our communication efforts.

CHAPTER NINE:

DEALING WITH DIFFICULT PEOPLE AND SITUATIONS

"To effectively communicate, we must realize that we are all different in the way we perceive the world and use this understanding as a guide to our communication with others."

— ANTHONY ROBBINS —

We've all been in unfortunate situations before where we've said something untoward. Whether we said the wrong thing maliciously or by accident, chances are that utterances lacked empathy to some extent.

A study published in the 2014 *Proceedings of the National Academy of Sciences* journal aimed to understand the effect prejudice has when communicating with different groups of people. The researchers hypothesized that positive intergroup contact would have a greater effect on reducing prejudice toward outgroups in contexts where intergroup relations are generally more negative. To test this hypothesis, the authors conducted a survey study with over 7,000 participants from various European countries, with interesting results.

The results showed that positive intergroup contact was associated with reduced prejudice toward outgroups (Christ et al., 2014). Overall, this study suggests that positive experiences with people can help reduce prejudice, but the effect may be influenced by the social context in which the contact occurs.

Judgment and lack of empathy lead conversations to "go wrong" most of the time. Even if we disagree with someone's opinion, there should be no room for misunderstandings if we constantly strive to understand where someone is coming from, right?

Well, if things were that simple, we'd hardly have the need for books on communication! Here's the rub, we don't know how someone will react to what we say. Even if we have good intentions and conduct our conversations with empathy, we are not in control of how another person will understand or respond to what we have to say. We can only control how we react.

Humans are wonderfully complex beings, and difficult situations will arise, whether we intend for them to or not. The virtual guarantee that difficult situations will eventually arise should not deter you from reaching out to people and forming new connections, not at all! Everything you've learned so far in this book has been designed to empower you to gracefully navigate the communication landscape. Difficult situations and people are just a part of that landscape. Fortunately, there are ways we can deal with difficult scenarios.

DEALING WITH BRASH INDIVIDUALS

Ever see someone smile and wave at you, only to discover to your dismay that the person was smiling and waving at someone behind you? This has happened to me quite a few times! It's a relatively harmless situation that arose because I misinterpreted the signals that person was sending. But what if I worked up the courage to approach the smiling and waving person only to be confronted by rude behavior? In situations like those, there are two ways we can deal with it (without silently wishing that the earth would swallow you whole in the moment).

Visualize this situation with me: We are at a coffee shop, and we spot someone who seems to be giving us all the right signals to approach. We work up the courage and approach them only to find out the person is not impressed with our efforts. We receive curt answers when we ask questions, and the situation is quickly becoming awkward. How do we handle a situation like that?

There's a quick fix if the person assumes our intentions. By apologizing for any offense caused and clarifying our intentions, we can clear up any misunderstandings early on. A simple "My apologies! I saw you sitting alone and wanted to have a chat; my name is..." should work. If the person softens, it is a good sign that we can continue the conversation, but if they continue to behave offhandedly or brashly, it is a sign that they want to be left alone. Walk away with your pride intact; that's what an empathetic communicator would do.

NAVIGATING HEATED DEBATES

Conversations are often started with the intention of it being a casual and friendly encounter, but not everything goes as planned and we may find ourselves in the middle of a red-hot debate. Feisty debates tend to arise when acceptance, understanding, and tolerance for another person's viewpoint are lacking. Without empathy we may start to judge, criticize, disrespect, or belittle others for their views, steering the conversation down a dangerous cliff. There's a good reason why certain topics (such as religion and politics) are considered taboo, as they can be very divisive. So, what do you do if you are dragged into a heated debate?

Let's say the person you're talking to holds very strong opinions about the political climate in a certain country. You try to share your opposing opinions with this person in a respectful manner, but your response prompts a defensive tirade about how your worldview is incorrect.

When divisive topics are debated, it is essential to remember that we can't control how other people will react to what we say. People can be easily offended by opposing views, especially if we haven't built a lot of rapport with them. Expect some backlash, even when you are absolutely empathetic and respectful in your approach when highly divisive topics are debated.

There are two ways we can deal with situations like these without them devolving into toxic shouting matches. The first way is to simply end the conversation politely and physically walk away. However, if we want to continue talking to the person, we might consider toning things down and laying some ground rules. Saying something like this should suffice:

"I respect your opinion, but you need to understand that my views are different. I am willing to continue this conversation, but you've got to respect that my opinions differ from yours."

If the person continues to be defensive and forceful with their opinions, it is best to end the conversation and walk away. However, if they acknowledge that they may have been acting unfairly and are willing to understand your views, it should be fine to continue the conversation. At this stage, it might be a good idea to suggest a change of topic to cool things down and foster some positive interaction.

HANDLING BAD CONVERSATIONS

Sometimes we encounter people whose beliefs don't match their actions. In psychology it is called "cognitive dissonance" and it can be a source of distress. The degree of distress depends on how well the person copes with the self-contradiction as well as the subject matter.

For example, a smoker might know all too well that their habit places them at an increased risk of developing cancer, but they still continue to smoke to manage their stress. With cognitive dissonance, a discrepancy arises between our values and what we feel at that particular moment (Tzeses, 2020).

It can become problematic when we start to rationalize our behaviors. Here's the thing, people don't easily give up a behavior, even if it is pointed out as being unhelpful. Instead, many people may choose to cling more tightly to their beliefs. So, what can we do about it?

The first step is to recognize that this tendency is present in most people, including yourself. Most people like to think they are rational, logical beings, but their behaviors don't always align with their beliefs.

The next step is to recognize the signs that someone is under the influence of cognitive dissonance. These signs include:

- Being surprised by new information, but not adjusting their viewpoint.

- An inability to correctly summarize other perspectives.

- Assuming that a person's intentions in the conversation are malicious.

- Focusing on your character or identity rather than the point you are making.

- Retreating quickly from the conversation without making concessions.

When we encounter someone who is debating us from the perspective of cognitive dissonance, it is best not to take the bait. You won't be able to convince the person otherwise, and, quite frankly, they won't be interested in hearing other views. What we should do is to find a way to build rapport. Tone things down and bring some levity to the situation. This will help with their defensiveness.

What if you encounter defensiveness and cognitive dissonance regularly? This is something that may be hard to hear, but it is entirely possible that you are inadvertently inviting these behaviors to surface with your mindset and approach. We often trigger this reaction in others if we treat conversations like something that can be won. If someone agrees with you, they inevitably come over to your side. When we treat conversations like this, the people we speak to will naturally be on the defensive. That's not the only mindset that triggers this reaction, though.

Sometimes we unconsciously expect people to adjust immediately to any new information that surfaces. I'll explain with an example. Sam and Mick are having a conversation about the meat industry. Sam admits that the meat industry might be treating animals unfairly. Mick quickly jumps on this new information and practically demands that Sam give up meat. How can he support an industry if he knows animals are being treated unfairly? Yet his reaction puts Sam on the defensive. What Mick failed to understand was that Sam simply needed time to come around. Rome was not built in one day, so it is unrealistic (and unfair) for us to expect others to immediately abandon their beliefs.

Another mindset that often triggers a defensive reaction is when we assume the role of a scorekeeper and hold people's past inconsistencies against them. When we turn our conversational partners into our opponents, they will behave defensively as a result. We need to convey the message that our intention is to understand and connect, not to combat.

If we try to have conversations with these mindsets, a communication breakdown is practically guaranteed. All is not lost, though! Whenever we feel ourselves entering these mindsets or treating the conversation like a game of chess, we need to remind ourselves what the goals of a true conversation are fostering understanding and building connections with people.

RESOLVING COMMUNICATION ISSUES IN CLOSE RELATIONSHIPS

Conversations can take a turn for the worst, even in close relationships. Managing conversations that go wrong is crucial in close relationships, as they can have a significant impact on us when issues are left unresolved.

The reason conversations go wrong in relationships is the same as with most other misunderstandings: due to a lack of empathy and judgment. Conflict can turn the happiest of relationships into a sour, tangled mess if it is not resolved effectively.

As with most things in life, there are healthy and unhealthy ways of going about this. Some people are conflict avoidant; that is, they would rather not deal with conflict situations and the discomfort of raising an issue. This is not a healthy way to deal with conflict and creates distance and resentment in a relationship. Some people keep score of the other person's past mistakes, while others tend to take all the blame in an attempt to fix things. These behaviors only lead to resentment.

There is one healthy way to solve conflict and safeguard the closeness of a relationship, and this is through compromise. Follow these steps closely and you'll be able to resolve misunderstandings in a healthy way.

STEP ONE: SPOT THE CAUSE

What do we do when our significant other or someone close to us says something hurtful? The first thing we need to do is to examine why that thing they said caused us to hurt. Maybe we wanted to buy a pair of shoes and our partner said to us "Are you really going to buy that?" This comment may make us feel upset because we felt like our significant other was passing judgment on our spending habits. When we understand why we are upset over what was said, it's time to look at the situation from their perspective. Perhaps our significant other already purchased a pair of shoes for us and wanted to save it as a surprise. Perhaps there was a different reason. The point is that we need to investigate why we felt hurt in the first place and then try to understand the situation from our own perspective and that of the other person.

STEP TWO: TALK ABOUT IT

When you examine both sides of the argument and arrive at an objective view of the scenario, it is time to talk about the issue. By stating the facts and owning our feelings we can talk about issues healthily without it escalating into an argument or sending the other person on the defensive.

Continuing with the shoe example, we might say something like this to our significant other:

"I wanted to talk to you about the earlier comment about me buying the shoes. When you asked this, I felt judged. Like I had done a bad thing."

STEP THREE: MOVING ON AND COMPROMISING

If you are the one in the wrong, the final step is to apologize. If you are the one who has been hurt, then the final step is to forgive the person. Afterward, both parties should come to a compromise.

When conversations go wrong because of something we said or did, we should make a genuine apology before trying to come up with any suggestions or solutions. A genuine apology entails a bit more than saying "I'm sorry." Heartfelt apologies are statements of what we are apologizing for, consideration for the impact our words or actions had, and how we plan to avoid hurting the other person's feelings in the future. Using the shoe example, a genuine apology would look something like this:

"I'm sorry for criticizing your spending habits. I can see now that doing so made you feel judged. I should have told you I had a surprise waiting for you at home. In the future, I'll be more open instead of making cryptic comments."

A true apology will contain no conditions, sarcasm, or other elements that will undermine it.

After we've apologized and forgiven, we need to reach a compromise or solution that makes both parties reasonably happy.

DEALING WITH DIFFICULT PEOPLE

We've all met people who have no scruples when it comes to crossing our boundaries. Setting boundaries in communication is important to ensure that your personal space, time, and feelings are respected by others. Setting boundaries is not a selfish act, it is about taking care of yourself and creating healthy, respectful connections with others (Boundaries: What Are They and How to Create Them, 2022). So how does one go about setting boundaries? The tips that follow will help you with that.

IDENTIFY YOUR BOUNDARIES
Take some time to think about what is important to you in terms of personal space, time, and emotions. What are the things that you are not comfortable with or that make you feel uneasy? Knowing your boundaries is the first step to setting them.

COMMUNICATE YOUR BOUNDARIES
Once you know your boundaries, communicate them clearly and assertively to the people you interact with.

Use "I" statements to express your feelings, and avoid blaming or criticizing others (Hailey, 2022).

BE CONSISTENT

Consistency is key when it comes to setting boundaries. Stick to your boundaries and don't let others violate them. This will help you build a reputation as someone who is firm and clear about their needs.

Keep in mind that communication is a two- or more-sided process, and it does not depend only on you. There are people you probably don't want or need to communicate with, and that is fine. Remember that if another person behaves badly, it is not a reflection of you, so don't take it personally. That being said, there are times when we have to deal with people who are behaving in less-than-ideal ways, and I'll share with you some ways to deal with these characters.

AGGRESSIVE PEOPLE

A technique that works well on aggressive and forceful individuals is to raise your hand into the stop sign. Simply raise your hand by your side to show the sign. Use this when a person is verbally attacking you or becoming too forceful. This nonverbal cue will politely signal that they've overstepped a boundary and need to stop.

COMPLAINERS

We've all been in a situation where we've met someone who complains without stopping! A fantastic way to deal with complainers is to agree with them and use the word "and" to gently suggest a solution. It will be incredibly hard to continue with a rant if someone agrees with you.

For example, if a person complains about the lack of service in a business, you could say something like this:

"I agree, the service was appalling, and if I were you, I'd be furious, too. It's simply not acceptable that nobody took the initiative to return your calls, and this is why I'm trying to sort this problem out now."

More often than not, ranting people may end up apologizing for their behavior.

THE MOTORMOUTH

Some people are avid talkers, which makes it very difficult for us to get a word in edgewise. If you find yourself in a situation like this and would like the opportunity to speak, you can use the "and" technique to politely interject without being rude. We need to exercise caution when doing this, as we are hijacking the conversation. Let's assume a person is passionately debating about different kinds of fruits, saying something like:

"There are many kinds of fruit I haven't even tried yet. From what I hear, durian is quite smelly..."

At this point, we can interject. All we need to do is link the conversation to what we want to talk about.

"...and really tasty! I've had durian many times before, and that's exactly why I love to travel to different countries and try local cuisine."

Openness and kindness should go hand in hand with strength and the ability to protect yourself and others. That's because others may perceive us as weak, and we will encounter totally different results as compared to what we wanted. Sometimes it is very necessary to be tough, not just pleasant and smiling, and that is perfectly fine! We all have our boundaries and need to enforce them from time to time.

CHAPTER NINE KEY TAKEAWAYS

✓ A lack of empathy and judgment are the root causes of communication going wrong on many occasions. Even if we disagree with someone's opinion there are ways to go about this that will not undermine the goal of communication, which is to build understanding and connections.

✓ A simple apology and clarification are sometimes enough to deal with a brash person. However, part of empathetic communication is knowing and understanding that not everyone wants to talk to everyone.

✓ Heated debates usually arise when empathy is lacking in a conversation, but we can deal with these difficult situations in a way that is respectful and effective.

✓ Sometimes our beliefs don't match our actions; this is called cognitive dissonance, and it can be a source of many communication difficulties. If we encounter cognitive dissonance frequently, we may be nurturing a mindset that encourages this behavior to surface in others.

✓ Resolving communication issues in close relationships is crucial to maintain the bonds of closeness. Identifying why we felt hurt, understanding the situation from our significant other's perspective, and giving a genuine apology can help to mend communication issues in a healthy way.

✓ Identifying and communicating our boundaries are important steps to ensuring that other people respect our time and feelings.

✓ If we encounter difficult people, there are ways of dealing politely with them.

CONCLUSION

"Communication is a skill that you can learn. It's like riding a bicycle or typing. If you're willing to work at it, you can rapidly improve the quality of every part of your life."

— BRIAN TRACY —

I've learned one undeniable truth: Effective communication is a skill that we learn, it is not something we are born with. Just like a flower growing in a pot, we'll need to nurture the basics of good communication and practice the principles we've learned for the best results.

Our communication skills will take some time to develop, just like that flower in the pot. But communication skills and the flower growing in the pot have a vital difference: A flower blooms when it is in season, whereas communication is a gift that keeps on giving. It is through the nurturing of these skills that we can attain our communication goals, become more confident in leading discussions, and find ways to build rapport and relationships with the people around us.

All of the tips and strategies shared in this book are based on the assumption that the goal of effective communication is to foster understanding. Through expressing confidence, showing our authentic selves, being empathetic listeners, reading body language, and adapting our approach to the situation, we are given the tools to better understand what the people around us are trying to say.

We also focused on starting conversations in different contexts and covered everything you need to know about approaching others and becoming charismatic and likable. Effective communication is essential for building and maintaining strong relationships, both personal and professional, so we've explored the various communication skills and strategies, such as active listening and empathy, needed to encourage strong relationships. We also learned about the barriers to communication, such as assumptions, and how to overcome them through awareness and understanding.

It is important to remember that communication is a two-way process, much like riding a tandem bicycle, and that both the sender and the receiver of the message have a role to play. By practicing the communication skills and strategies outlined in this book, you'll gain the skills needed to improve relationships, enhance problem-solving abilities, and achieve greater success in all aspects of life.

Of course, success is a marathon, not a sprint! So, remember to take a break and recharge whenever you need it. Achieving a good balance between your personal and social time is a good way to prevent some of the stress associated with communicating. Self-care is not selfish, and we can't pour from an empty cup, so taking care of ourselves is an important (and often overlooked) step in improving our communication skills.

As we work on our skills, it's a guarantee that there will be fantastic failures and interesting blunders. Remember, we're all humans, and nobody was born a great communicator. It's perfectly fine to laugh at your mistakes. Change takes time, so don't be in a rush. You've got this!

Now that you've got all the skills you need, there's only one thing left to do: Go out there and start a conversation!

If this book was helpful, I'd love to hear from you! Whether you purchased this book online or borrowed it from a friend, let me know what your thoughts are by leaving a review on Amazon.

REFERENCES

56 Great Conversation Quotes To Help You Talk It Out. (n.d.). Kidadl. https://kidadl.com/quotes/great-conversation-quotes-to-help-you-talk-it-out

56 Inspiring Team Communication Quotes To Motivate Your Team. (2021). Indeed Career Guide. https://www.indeed.com/career-advice/career-development/team-communication-quotes#:~:text=%22Communication%20%E2%80%93%20the%20human%20connection%20%E2%80%93

75 Communication Quotes and Sayings to Strengthen Relationships. (2021, March 24). Everyday Power. https://everydaypower.com/communication-quotes-and-sayings/

Baker, T., & Warren, A. (2015). Active Listening Can Make Other People Better Communicators Too. Conversations at Work, 160–175. https://doi.org/10.1057/9781137534187_11

Baldoni, J. (2014). Really Smart People Never Show Off How Smart They Are. LinkedIn. https://www.linkedin.com/pulse/20140614152839-9692147-really-smart-people-never-show-off-how-smart-they-are

Bindamnan, A. (2023). 3 Tips to Overcome Shyness. Psychology Today. https://www.psychologytoday.com/us/blog/zero-generation-students/202302/3-tips-to-overcome-shyness

Boris, V. (2017, December 20). What Makes Storytelling So Effective For Learning? Harvard Business Publishing. https://www.harvardbusiness.org/what-makes-storytelling-so-effective-for-learning/

Borthwick, D. (2022). How to Talk to Anybody - Learn The Secrets To Small Talk, Business, Management, Sales & Social Skills & How to Make Real Friends (Communication Skills).

Boundaries: What are they and how to create them. (2022, February 25). University of Illinois Chicago. https://wellnesscenter.uic.edu/news-stories/boundaries-what-are-they-and-how-to-create-them/#:~:text=Setting%20boundaries%20is%20a%20form

Brimble, L. (2021, April 20). Nearly half of Brits hide their true personality from loved ones, study finds. Express.co.uk. https://www.express.co.uk/life-style/life/1425523/half-britons-hide-true-personality-from-loved-ones-study-finds

Burger, E., & Neale, M. A. (2018). The art of using cold reading to connect with people. Harvard Business Review. https://hbr.org/2018/02/the-art-of-using-cold-reading-to-connect-with-people

Can You Learn How to Be Charismatic. (2020, December 22). Healthline. https://www.healthline.com/health/how-to-be-charismatic

Carnegie, D. (2018). How To Win Friends And Influence People. Simon & Schuster. (Original work published 1936)

Carney, D. R., Cuddy, A. J. C., & Yap, A. J. (2010). Power posing: Brief nonverbal displays affect neuroendocrine levels and risk tolerance. Psychological Science, 21(10), 1363–1368. https://doi.org/10.1177/0956797610383437

Charisma Quotes (217 quotes). (n.d.). Www.goodreads.com. Retrieved March 1, 2023, from https://www.goodreads.com/quotes/tag/charisma#:~:text=%E2%80%9CBut%20charisma%20only%20wins%20people

Christ, O., Schmid, K., Lolliot, S., Swart, H., Stolle, D., Tausch, N., Al Ramiah, A., Wagner, U., Vertovec, S., & Hewstone, M. (2014).

Contextual effect of positive intergroup contact on outgroup prejudice. Proceedings of the National Academy of Sciences, 111(11), 3996–4000. https://doi.org/10.1073/pnas.1320901111

Christopher Voss Quotes. (n.d.). BrainyQuote. Retrieved February 22, 2023, from https://www.brainyquote.com/authors/christopher-voss-quotes

Conversational Anxiety. (n.d.). National Social Anxiety Center. Retrieved February 16, 2023, from https://nationalsocialanxietycenter.com/social-anxiety/conversational-anxiety/#:~:text=STRENGTH%3A%20FREE%20ASSOCIATING.

Doyle, A. (2021, March 13). These are the communication skills employers look for in employees. The Balance. https://www.thebalancemoney.com/communication-skills-list-2063779

Dunne, C. (2019, May 8). 40 Team Communication Quotes to Inspire Your Team. Tameday. https://www.tameday.com/team-communication-quotes/

Ekman, P., & Friesen, W. V. (1969). The Repertoire of Nonverbal Behavior: Categories, Origins, Usage, and Coding. Semiotica, 1(1). https://doi.org/10.1515/semi.1969.1.1.49

Fine, D. (2014). The Fine Art Of Small Talk. Hachette UK.

Ghazavi, Z., Feshangchi, S., Alavi, M., & Keshvari, M. (2016). Effect of a Family-Oriented Communication Skills Training Program on Depression, Anxiety, and Stress in Older Adults: A Randomized Clinical Trial. Nursing and Midwifery Studies, Inpress(Inpress). https://doi.org/10.17795/nmsjournal28550

Goldsmith, M. (n.d.). Instead of Feedback, Try Feedforward to Boost Team Performance. In University of Iowa. Retrieved March 1, 2023, from https://hr.uiowa.edu/sites/hr.uiowa.edu/files/2022-10/FeedForward.pdf

Gordon, J. (2022). Understand Yourself Before Communicating - Explained. The Business Professor, LLC. https://thebusinessprofessor.com/en_US/communications-negotiations/understand-yourself-before-communicating

Hailey, L. (2022, April 15). How to Set Boundaries: 5 Ways to Draw the Line Politely. Science of People. https://www.scienceofpeople.com/how-to-set-boundaries/

Hall, J. A., Coats, E. J., & Lavonia Smith LeBeau. (2005). Nonverbal Behavior and the Vertical Dimension of Social Relations: A Meta-Analysis. Psychological Bulletin, 131(6), 898–924. https://doi.org/10.1037/0033-2909.131.6.898

Hinkle, D. E., & Wolff, R. (1957). The Power of Enthusiasm in Social Interaction. Journal of Personality, 25(2), 213–225.

Hopkins, R. (2020, October 23). Some reflections on the difference between "Yes, but" and "Yes, and." Rob Hopkins. https://www.robhopkins.net/2020/10/23/some-reflections-on-the-difference-between-yes-but-and-yes-and/#:~:text=Saying%20%E2%80%9Cyes%2C%20but%E2%80%9D%20allows

Improving Self-Esteem. (2011). Skills You Need. https://www.skillsyouneed.com/ps/self-esteem.html

Jim Rohn Quotes. (n.d.). BrainyQuote. Retrieved February 28, 2023, from https://www.brainyquote.com/quotes/jim_rohn_165073?src=t_commun ication

Jost, J. T., Banaji, M. R., & Nosek, B. A. (2004). A Decade of System Justification Theory: Accumulated Evidence of Conscious and Unconscious Bolstering of the Status Quo. Political Psychology, 25(6), 881–919. https://www.jstor.org/stable/3792282

Kardas, M., Kumar, A., & Epley, N. (2021). Overly shallow?: Miscalibrated expectations create a barrier to deeper conversation. Journal of Personality and Social Psychology. https://doi.org/10.1037/pspa0000281

Koudenburg, N., Postmes, T., & Gordijn, E. H. (2011). Disrupting the flow: How brief silences in group conversations affect social needs. Journal of Experimental Social Psychology, 47(2), 512–515. https://doi.org/10.1016/j.jesp.2010.12.006

Lowndes, L. (2003). How to talk to anyone : 92 little tricks for big success in relationships. Contemporary Books.

Martin, S. (2017, April 24). Inspirational Quotes to Help You Know Yourself and Live Authentically. Psych Central. https://psychcentral.com/blog/imperfect/2017/04/inspirational-quotes-to-help-you-know-yourself-and-live-authenticity#2

Mastroianni, A. M., Gilbert, D. T., Cooney, G., & Wilson, T. D. (2021). Do conversations end when people want them to? Proceedings of the National Academy of Sciences, 118(10). https://doi.org/10.1073/pnas.2011809118

Matsumoto, D., & Hwang, H. C. (2017). Methodological Issues Regarding Cross-Cultural Studies of Judgments of Facial Expressions. Emotion Review, 9(4), 375–382. https://doi.org/10.1177/1754073916679008

Mehl, M. R., Vazire, S., Ramirez-Esparza, N., Slatcher, R. B., & Pennebaker, J. W. (2007). Are Women Really More Talkative Than Men? Science, 317(5834), 82–82. https://doi.org/10.1126/science.1139940

Mehrabian, A., & Ferris, S. R. (1967). Inference of Attitudes from Nonverbal Communication in Two channels. Journal of Consulting Psychology, 31(3), 248–252. https://doi.org/10.1037/h0024648

Mehrabian's Communication Model. (n.d.). Mind Tools. https://www.mindtools.com/ao9kek8/mehrabians-communication-model

Mendonsa, S. (2018, February 9). Mirroring Technique In Psychology: Pacing And Leading To Influence Others. Master Influencer Magazine. https://master-influencer.com/pacing-and-leading-using-mimicry-and-mirroring-to-influence-and-lead-others/

Methot, J. R., Rosado-Solomon, E. H., Downes, P., & Gabriel, A. S. (2020). Office Chit-Chat as a Social Ritual: The Uplifting Yet Distracting Effects of Daily Small Talk at Work. Academy of Management Journal, 64(5). https://doi.org/10.5465/amj.2018.1474

Mindnatic. (2022). How to Talk to Anyone and Everyone: Hold Better Conversation, Master Small Talk and Improve Social Skills (Communication Skills and Charisma Development) (pp. 45–46). Mindnatic.

Navarro, J., & Karlins, M. (2015). What every BODY is saying : an ex-FBI agent's guide to speed-reading people. Harper Collins.

Okuhira, M. A., & Yoshimura, Y. (2016). Communicative Functions of Silence and Implications for Psychological Well-Being: A Narrative Review. Frontiers in Psychology, 7, 18–57.

Orth, U., & Robins, R. W. (2022). Is high self-esteem beneficial? Revisiting a classic question. American Psychologist, 77(1), 5–17. https://doi.org/10.1037/amp0000922

Parker, S. K., Axtell, C. M., & Turner, N. (2001). Designing a safer workplace: Importance of job autonomy, communication quality, and supportive supervisors. Journal of Occupational Health Psychology, 6(3), 211–228. https://doi.org/10.1037//1076-8998.6.3.211

Pause. (n.d.). National Center for Voice and Speech. https://www.ncvs.org/ncvs/tutorials/voiceprod/tutorial/pause.html

Primack, B. A., Shensa, A., Sidani, J. E., Whaite, E. O., Lin, L. yi, Rosen, D., Colditz, J. B., Radovic, A., & Miller, E. (2017). Social Media Use and Perceived Social Isolation Among Young Adults in the U.S. American Journal of Preventive Medicine, 53(1), 1–8. https://doi.org/10.1016/j.amepre.2017.01.010

Reading Improves Memory, Concentration and Stress. (2016, December 10). Northcentral University. https://www.ncu.edu/blog/reading-improves-memory-concentration-and-stress#gref

Riegel, D. G. (2018, October 12). Stop Complaining About Your Colleagues Behind Their Backs. Harvard Business Review. https://hbr.org/2018/10/stop-complaining-about-your-colleagues-behind-their-backs#:~:text=Like%20the%20erosion%20of%20trust

Sasaki, N., Somemura, H., Nakamura, S., Yamamoto, M., Isojima, M., Shinmei, I., Horikoshi, M., & Tanaka, K. (2017). Effects of Brief Communication Skills Training for Workers Based on the Principles of Cognitive Behavioral Therapy: A Randomized Controlled Trial. Journal of Occupational and Environmental Medicine, 59(1), 61–66. https://doi.org/10.1097/JOM.0000000000000924

Schwartz, M. (2019). The Power of Authentic Self-Esteem. Psychology Today. https://www.psychologytoday.com/za/blog/shift-mind/201911/the-power-authentic-self-esteem

Scott, E. (2020). Improving Your Communication Skills to Reduce Stress. Verywell Mind. https://www.verywellmind.com/the-stress-of-poor-communication-with-others-4154175

Segal, J., Smith, M., Robinson, L., & Boose, G. (2022, December 5). Nonverbal Communication and Body Language. HelpGuide. https://www.helpguide.org/articles/relationships-communication/nonverbal-communication.htm

SHIGEMI, J., MINO, Y., TSUDA, T., BABAZONO, A., & AOYAMA, H. (1997). The Relationship between Job Stress and Mental Health at Work. INDUSTRIAL HEALTH, 35(1), 29–35. https://doi.org/10.2486/indhealth.35.29

Smith, E. S., Geissler, S. A., Schallert, T., & Lee, H. J. (2013). The role of central amygdala dopamine in disengagement behavior. Behavioral Neuroscience, 127(2), 164–174. https://doi.org/10.1037/a0031043

Tamir, D. I., & Mitchell, J. P. (2012). Disclosing information about the self is intrinsically rewarding. Proceedings of the National Academy of Sciences, 109(21), 8038–8043. https://doi.org/10.1073/pnas.1202129109

The Difference Between Empathy and Sympathy. (2022, October 11). Psychiatric Medical Care. https://www.psychmc.com/blogs/empathy-vs-sympathy#:~:text=Empathy%20is%20shown%20in%20how

The Language of Eye Movements Part Two. (2011, August 11). Eurisko Design. https://euriskodesign.com/the-language-of-eye-movements-part-two/#:~:text=The%20social%20gaze%20would%20take

The Mindsets of a Great Communicator. (2021). Group Sixty. https://www.groupsixty.com/ideas-blog/2021/5/5/the-mindsets-of-a-great-communicator

Thompson, S. (2017, August 10). 8 Elements of Confident Body Language. Virtualspeech.com; VirtualSpeech. https://virtualspeech.com/blog/8-elements-of-confident-body-language

Tipper, C. M., Signorini, G., & Grafton, S. T. (2015). Body language in the brain: constructing meaning from expressive movement. Frontiers in Human Neuroscience, 9. https://doi.org/10.3389/fnhum.2015.00450

Tzeses, J. (2020, November 30). Cognitive Dissonance: What It Is and Why It Matters. Psycom. https://www.psycom.net/cognitive-dissonance

Vallín, E. N. (2022, June 20). 9 hand gestures easily misunderstood abroad. Deafumbrella. https://www.deafumbrella.com/post/9-hand-gestures-easily-misunderstood-abroad1

Van Edwards, V. (n.d.). People who are "confident and interesting" always avoid these 5 mistakes, says public speaking expert. CNBC. https://www.cnbc.com/2022/04/27/avoid-these-mistakes-if-you-want-to-sound-more-confident-and-interesting-says-public-speaking-expert.html

van Edwards, V. (2021, January 6). Feet Behavior - The Untapped Body Language You Should Know. Science of People. https://www.scienceofpeople.com/feet-body-language/

van Tilburg, W. A. P., Igou, E. R., & Panjwani, M. (2022). Boring People: Stereotype Characteristics, Interpersonal Attributions, and Social Reactions. Personality and Social Psychology Bulletin, 014616722210791. https://doi.org/10.1177/01461672221079104

Vardhman, S., Goyal, S., & Vashist, A. (2019). The Power of Silence and Pause in Conversational Intelligence. Journal of Advances in Linguistics and Literature, 9(1), 43–48.

Voss, C. (2021). How to Use the 7-38-55 Rule to Negotiate Effectively. MasterClass. https://www.masterclass.com/articles/how-to-use-the-7-38-55-rule-to-negotiate-effectively

Weger, H., Castle Bell, G., Minei, E. M., & Robinson, M. C. (2014). The relative effectiveness of active listening in initial interactions. International Journal of Listening, 28(1), 13–31.

Williams, J. W. (2021). How to Talk to Anyone About Anything: Improve Your Social Skills, Master Small Talk, Connect Effortlessly, and Make Real Friends. In Amazon. https://www.amazon.com/Talk-Anyone-About-Anything-Communication-ebook/dp/B091367FRH/ref=sr_1_5?crid=2FOIOKNFNFIQ0&keyword

s=how+to+talk+to+anyone&qid=1675106774&s=books&sprefix=how
+to+talk+to+anyone%2Cstripbooks-intl-ship%2C220&sr=1-5

Wrench, J. S., Punyanunt-Carter, N. M., & Thweatt, K. S. (2020).
Interpersonal Communication: A Mindful Approach to Relationships.
Open SUNY Textbooks.
https://knightscholar.geneseo.edu/cgi/viewcontent.cgi?article=1028&co
ntext=oer-ost

Made in the USA
Las Vegas, NV
07 November 2023